CW00524214

Attributions in Action

Attributions in Action

A Practical Approach to Coding Qualitative Data

Anthony G. Munton
Thomas Coram Research Unit, Institute of Education,
University of London, London, UK

Joanne Silvester
Department of Psychology, City University, London, UK

Peter Stratton
Leeds Family Therapy and Research Centre, School of Psychology,
University of Leeds, Leeds, UK

Helga Hanks
Department of Clinical & Health Psychology, St. James's University Hospital,
Leeds, UK

JOHN WILEY & SONS
Chichester · New York · Weinheim · Brisbane · Singapore · Toronto

Copyright © 1999 by John Wiley & Sons Ltd,
Baffins Lane, Chichester,
West Sussex PO19 1UD, England

National   01243 779777
International (+44) 1243 779777
e-mail (for orders and customer service enquiries):
cs-books@wiley.co.uk
Visit our Home Page on http://www.wiley.co.uk
            or http://www.wiley.com

Other Wiley Editorial Offices

John Wiley & Sons, Inc., 605 Third Avenue,
New York, NY 10158-0012, USA

WILEY-VCH Verlag GmbH, Pappelallee 3,
D-69469 Weinheim, Germany

Jacaranda Wiley Ltd, 33 Park Road, Milton,
Queensland 4064, Australia

John Wiley & Sons (Asia) Pte Ltd, 2 Clementi Loop #02-01,
Jin Xing Distripark, Singapore 129809

John Wiley & Sons (Canada) Ltd, 22 Worcester Road,
Rexdale, Ontario M9W 1L1, Canada

British Library Cataloguing in Publication Data

A catalogue record for this book is available from the British Library

ISBN 0-471-98216-4

Typeset in 11/13pt Palatino by Dorwyn Ltd, Rowlands Castle, Hants.
Printed and bound in Great Britain by Bookcraft (Bath) Ltd, Midsomer Norton, Somerset
This book is printed on acid-free paper responsibly manufactured from sustainable forestry, in which at least two trees are planted for each one used for paper production.

Contents

About the authors

Tony Munton is a Research Officer in the Thomas Coram Research Unit at the Institute of Education, University of London. He obtained a BA (Hons.) in Psychology and Sociology from the University of Leeds in 1980, and a PhD from the Leeds Family Therapy Research Centre, University of Leeds in 1987. His doctoral research concerned the attitudes and beliefs of families as they dealt with potential stressors. Much of this work with families involved the use of qualitative research tools, and development of the Leeds Attributional Coding System with Peter Stratton and the LFTRC team. From Leeds he moved to the MRC/ESRC Social and Applied Psychology Unit at the University of Sheffield to undertake research, both qualitative and quantitative, into the impact of job change on family life.

At the Institute of Education, much of his current work is policy relevant research for government departments. His research interests include childcare provision, families, and the implications of evidence-based approaches for the social sciences.

Jo Silvester is a Lecturer in Organisational Psychology at City University. She completed her BSc at the University of York, a PhD at the University of Leeds and an MSc in Occupational Psychology at Birkbeck College, University of London. After working as a consultant organisational psychologist with commercial organisations for a number of years, she returned to academia and has held lecturerships at the University of Leeds and the University of Wales Swansea. She has published in the areas of selection decisions, unfair discrimination and organisational culture. Her current research and consultancy interests concern psychological factors contributing to sales performance and customer care.

Peter Stratton is a Senior Lecturer in the School of Psychology at Leeds University. His research uses the intensive qualitative methodology of the LACS to provide practical solutions for a broad range of issues. The applications in marketing and organisations are conducted through his company, The Psychology Business Ltd, which specialises in applying state-of-the-art psychology to commercial problems. From its base in attribution theory the company has created new approaches to relationship marketing, psychosegmentation, international comparisons, family decision processes, branding and risk prediction. In parallel with this research is his work as an accredited family therapist. He is Director of the Leeds Family Therapy and Research Centre in which the LACS was originally developed. The Centre provides an MSc in systemic family therapy and applies the LACS, and a related coding system for attachments, to issues of family difficulties, blaming, child abuse, and the effectiveness of systemic therapy. He is Joint Editor of *Human Systems: The Journal of Systemic Consultation and Management*.

Helga Hanks is a Consultant Clinical Psychologist in Psychotherapy and Family Therapy with a special responsibility in Child Abuse at St James's University Hospital, Leeds, Honorary Senior Lecturer, Department of Psychology, Leeds University, and Clinical Director of the Leeds Family Therapy and Research Centre at Leeds University. She is a founder member of that Centre and has been actively involved in the development of the LACS since the early 1980s. Her work both with children who have been abused and families has involved clinical work and research. She has applied the LACS in her research about the beliefs in families and about how they function and in the area of child abuse, researching into the beliefs of parents when their children have been abused. She has published widely and been Associate Editor of *Child Abuse Review* between 1992 and 1998 she is also a member of the editorial board of *Human Systems: The Journal of Systemic Consultation and Management*.

Preface

Ten years ago, the first coding manual of the Leeds Attributional Coding System (LACS) was written (Stratton *et al.*, 1988). It described a system for coding attributions expressed during natural discourse. The method was developed over several years by researchers and clinicians at the Leeds Family Therapy Research Centre (LFTRC), under the watchful eye of Peter Stratton. Since the manual was first published, the LACS has been used by researchers, clinicians and practitioners all over the world.

While travelling back from a LACS symposium held in Indianapolis, USA, two of the authors started talking about the need to rewrite the manual. We were particularly keen to expand it to provide detailed examples of how the method had been applied over the last 10 years. Peter Stratton and Helga Hanks, two of the original development team who have been using the LACS extensively since its inception, had also been discussing a similar project. Once we got together, we found we had all had many requests for details concerning application of the LACS method. Attribution theory remains popular among social scientists, along with the demand for a method of coding causal beliefs that does not rely on paper and pencil tests.

We have written this book in response to the considerable interest shown in the LACS over the last decade. Our aim has been to produce a manual that will be readily accessible to people who want to use the LACS in applied research. At the same time, we have tried to give the reader a flavour of the variety of settings in which the extraction and coding of causal beliefs have provided insights into many different aspects of human behaviour.

Acknowledgements

Development of the LACS owes something to many of our colleagues. In particular we would like to acknowledge the value of conversations we have had with Fiona Anderson, Charles Antaki, Chris Brewin, Frank Fincham, Dorothy Heard, Chris Peterson and Martin Seligman. Among those who have been involved with the current volume, our thanks are due to Michelle New.

1

Introduction

Anyone looking through academic journals in psychology over the last 10 years could not help but be impressed by the number of papers mentioning 'attributions' or 'attribution theory'. Clinical, educational, medical and occupational psychology are just some areas in which practitioners and researchers alike have applied attribution theory to their work. This chapter sets out to do three things. First, we will explain how attribution theory relates to behavioural and cognitive theories of learning; second, we will explain what attributions are; and, finally, we will show how attribution theory has been applied to practical problems.

ATTRIBUTIONS AND UNDERSTANDING BEHAVIOUR

Attribution theory offers a method for understanding human behaviour. For example, attributions can help us to understand why someone is depressed, why someone is feeling under strain at work, or even why someone chooses to buy one brand of chocolate cake instead of another. Depression, strain and purchasing are all behaviours that include learned elements of one sort or another. For our purposes we can define learning as a relatively permanent change in behaviour that occurs as a result of experience. Understanding human behaviour is often a question of understanding the learning process. The purpose of this section is to explore how attribution theory fits into different theories of learning.

Psychological theories of learning can be placed into two broad categories: cognitive and behavioural. Cognitive theories emphasise the importance of thought in predicting behaviour.

Behavioural approaches, on the other hand, explain behaviour in terms of conditioning; thinking processes play no significant part in behavioural theories of learning. Attribution theory includes elements of both cognitive and behavioural explanations of learning.

The behaviourists have two major theories of learning: classical and operant conditioning. First identified by Ivan Pavlov, a physiologist, classical conditioning showed how automatic or reflex type behaviours could be manipulated. Pavlov noticed that his dogs started to salivate when they saw the bucket from which they were normally fed. The buckets signalled the arrival of food, and the dogs began to salivate in anticipation. Next, Pavlov tried to teach the dogs to associate something other than the bucket with food. In his best-known experiment he used a bell. When the bucket appeared, a bell rang. The dogs salivated as normal. Before long, the dogs learned to associate the bucket with the bell. Consequently, ringing a bell without a bucket being in sight could make the dogs salivate. Pavlov concluded that we could explain learning through associations.

Classical conditioning has many practical uses, particularly in clinical psychology. We can sometimes explain addictions with classical conditioning. For example, drinking, taking drugs, or shopping can all become addictive behaviours. In each case the behaviours have been associated with pleasant outcomes. Moderate amounts of alcohol often increase feelings of well-being and sociability. Addicts associate pleasant feelings and drinking, until they cannot enjoy themselves without a drink. To extinguish addictive behaviour requires the addict to learn a different response to a particular stimulus. Aversion therapy is one example of a behaviour therapy. Widely used in the treatment of alcohol and drug abuse, it involves the application of an emetic, a drug that causes people to vomit. The treatment follows a simple classical conditioning pattern. The clinician gives people an emetic drug while also giving them a drink. In time they associate drinking with feeling sick. This unpleasant association encourages them to avoid alcohol.

The other major behavioural theory that deals with learning is operant conditioning. Operant conditioning deals with the way in which we learn voluntary behaviours. It is based on one of the simplest yet most influential laws in psychological science, Thorndike's 'Law of Effect'. The law of effect states that 'if a certain response has pleasant consequences it is more likely than other responses to occur again in the same circumstances'. Subsequently B.F. Skinner introduced the idea of reinforcement into the definition. This became the principle of operant conditioning: 'Behaviour which is reinforced tends to be repeated, behaviour which is not reinforced tends to die out or be extinguished.'

Staying with practical applications in clinical psychology, some therapeutic techniques use the principles of operant conditioning in the treatment of problem behaviours. Clinical interventions based on operant conditioning principles use the same reasoning outlined earlier. Abnormal behaviour is the result of faulty learning. We have rewarded or reinforced the undesirable behaviour at some point, and that is why it persists. Find out what the rewards and reinforcers are, and the behaviour can be changed. For example, imagine the parents of a child with severe temper tantrums. According to the principles of operant conditioning, we must be reinforcing the child's bad behaviour, otherwise he or she would not repeat it. The therapist explores the circumstances in which the temper tantrums occur and how parents respond to it. For example, parents will sometimes try to distract a badly behaved child by giving it a sweet, a biscuit or a toy to play with. The child learns to associate loss of temper with getting a reward. They are reinforcing the child's bad behaviour.

In this example, the behaviour therapist might recommend to the parents that they change this pattern of interaction between themselves and their child. They should ignore temper tantrums, not reinforce them in any circumstances. Only when the child behaves well should parents offer a reward. Rewarding good behaviour makes it more likely that the child will behave well in future.

For the behaviourists, thought or cognition has little to do with the learning process. The opposing view is that finding out what people think is more important than simply observing behaviour. Freud and the psychoanalytic theorists promoted the importance of thought. Freud emphasised the importance of talking to his patients about their thoughts and feelings, trying to understanding how they perceived themselves and their world. Psychoanalytic theory claimed that changing behaviour without challenging the reasons that lay behind it would only lead to the emergence of new, unwanted behaviour. When his patients found it difficult to recall details of their past, Freud used hypnosis to help them. Gradually he developed his ideas about conscious and subconscious processes, defence mechanisms and his now famous Trinity of id, ego and superego.

We have labelled this tradition of interest in thought *cognitive psychology*. For a long time the cognitivists and behaviourists sat in opposing corners, each arguing that the other's perspective was either unscientific or unimaginative. However, in more recent times, probably starting during the 1950s, a third alternative arose. Enter the cognitive-behaviourists.

Cognitive-behavioural theories of learning apply a different interpretation to the same sequence of stimuli and responses described by the behaviourists. Introducing the notion of mental models achieves this. Using models to predict what may or may not happen in reality is a technique commonly used by engineers, designers and scientists. A civil engineer would not build a new bridge without first constructing a model to see how the structure would behave under a variety of conditions. The designer of a new aeroplane first builds a model to predict performance. These models are representations of reality, used to make predictions about what might happen in the real world. The cognitive-behaviourists argue that people construct mental models of reality in just the same way. Mental models are representations of the world and how it operates, and are used to make predictions about reality. For example, someone's internal model of the world may incorporate information about light switches. In this model, flicking a switch causes a light to come on. This relationship between switches and lights is a feature of this mental model of the world. It enables the person to make useful predictions about what to do when one enters a dark room.

This idea of mental models is consistent with behavioural explanations of learning. The difference comes in the explanation of exactly what we learn. In classical conditioning explanations, a new stimulus is associated with existing response. The subject learns to salivate (existing response) when he or she hears a bell (a new stimulus). Thought is not involved. The process is automatic.

We sometimes call this S–R or stimulus–response learning. Cognitive-behavioural explanations claim that this is too mechanical a description. Instead, they use the mental model notion. The subject learns that the old stimulus (the food) usually follows the new stimulus (the bell). Because he or she expects food, the response is salivation. Even when the food does not appear, salivation still takes place. The subject now has a mental model in which the appearance of food follows the sound of a bell. We know this as S–S or stimulus–stimulus learning.

Cognitive-behavioural approaches offer a more flexible interpretation of learning. People can build and modify mental models without concrete experience. For example, a child can learn that fires are dangerous without having to get burned. Teaching road safety is a simple but practical example of the process. A child does not have to be involved in a traffic accident to learn about the dangers of running into a busy road. Through teaching, children can get an internal model of the world in which moving cars are dangerous objects. We modify the child's internal model of the world to cause a change in behaviour.

Using the cognitive-behavioural interpretation, we can understand learning and behaviour in terms of the internal mental models that people have. To understand and predict human behaviour, we need to know something about people's internal mental models of their world. In particular, knowing how people see the relationship between events (and behaviours) and causes can be very useful.

Take, for example, parents of a child with temper tantrums. A clinical psychologist can offer an effective solution using the principles of operant conditioning. The solution involves the parents changing the way in which they respond to their child's behaviour. The success of this strategy depends on the parents being willing and able to change the way they treat their child. They may, however, believe that some genetic fault or the child's star sign causes the tantrums. Then, they are unlikely to believe that changing their behaviour will make any difference. In such circumstances, the clinical psychologist may face problems in trying to modify the child's behaviour.

Uncovering what people believe about events and their causes is a very useful way into understanding and predicting behaviour. Attributions, or causal explanations, tell us what a person thinks about events and their causes. It is this fact that makes attributions an important and powerful tool in the search to understand human behaviour.

To summarise, attributions are beliefs about causality. They are a way of classifying or categorising thoughts about events and their causes. As this book will show, categorising thoughts about causality can be of great practical significance when trying to understand and change behaviour.

WHAT IS AN ATTRIBUTION?

Attribution theory is concerned with the thoughts people have about events and what causes them. An attribution is an expression of the way a person thinks about the relationship between a cause and an outcome. For example, imagine someone asking why you are a psychologist. You might reply, 'Because I have always been interested in people.' You have made an attribution. You have associated an event (being a psychologist) with a cause (an interest in people). The following are a few more examples: 'I look stupid in these green trousers.' We link a behaviour (looking stupid) with a cause (wearing green trousers). 'I can't live with him because he is so untidy around the house.' We link an outcome (not being able to live with a friend) to a cause (he is untidy). 'All these cars make the city so unhealthy.' We link a state of affairs (the city being unhealthy) with the cause (too many cars). We make attributions about behaviour, both our own and other people's, about events, and about anything that requires a causal explanation. The nature versus nurture debate that has so preoccupied psychologists, concerns the attribution of behaviour to genes, environment, or both. Whatever the context, an attribution involves some event, behaviour or characteristic that is being coupled with a possible cause.

Given this description, it will come as no surprise that attributions are also labelled 'causal explanations'. However, philosophers have identified problems with defining attributions as causal explanations. A description of an event and the circumstances leading up to that event need not always be a causal explanation. An important difference exists between causal explanations and reasoned explanations.

Reasons and causes are two distinct forms of explanation. The problem for attribution theory is how, or even whether, to distinguish between the two. For example, take the statement 'I went to bed early last night because I was tired'. Did tiredness *cause* the speaker to go to bed, or was tiredness the *reason* for the speaker going to bed? Does it matter whether this is a cause or a reason as far as attribution theory is concerned? If it does matter, how can we tell the difference between a reason and a cause?

No simple formula exists for distinguishing between reasons and causes. However, this has not deterred several people from maintaining that such a difference does exist. We can sum the dilemma up quite neatly using a quotation from the philosopher William James:

> *The word* cause *is, in short, an altar to an unknown god; an empty pedestal still marking the place of a hoped-for statue.*

The history of philosophy is littered with attempts to resolve this issue. Aristotle, Plato, Hobbes, Descartes, Hempel and Habermas have all been brought in to justify one position or another.

We can probably reduce the arguments to one of two positions. Some argue that reasons and causes are most definitely two different kinds of explanation. Furthermore, they assert that recognising this distinction is vitally important for attribution theorists. On the other hand, some feel that we can, indeed should, ignore the issue if attribution theory is ever to make a valuable scientific contribution.

Those who can distinguish between reasons and causes say that the difference is quite straightforward. A cause is something that brings about a change, while a reason is something for which we bring about a change. However, making this distinction in practice is not so straightforward. Take the following example: 'I had a drink because I was thirsty.' Is the speaker in this example providing a *cause* for their having a drink, or providing a *reason* for drinking? Applying the reason–cause distinction, the action (drinking) most definitely brought about some change (thirst was quenched). Accordingly, the statement must be a causal explanation. However, we can also say that the speaker took a drink to fulfil some purpose (to quench thirst). We can also describe the statement as a reasoned explanation.

Given the same example, others would argue that the action (drinking) would not have taken place unless the person concerned had some reason to do so. Therefore the change (thirst being quenched) was brought about for a reason. So, both reasons and causes can be responsible for bringing about change. So we uncover a fatal inconsistency in the reason–cause distinction.

This is only one of many similar debates about attributions to be found in philosophy. Unfortunately none has produced a clear way of distinguishing between reasons and causes that can deal successfully (i.e. consistently) with specific examples.

Reasons and causes are probably indistinguishable for the purposes of using attribution theory. If we treat them as two separate forms of explanation, we would have to revise completely many attributional theories. We know this position as the 'reasons–explanations' view of attributions. Since attribution theory is dealing with explanation in a general sense, any distinction that might exist is of no great significance.

Where does this leave those trying to apply attributional theories to real-life situations? What are we looking for in an interview transcript? One of the most straightforward definitions of an attribution comes from the English philosopher Braithwaite, who commented that:

> an explanation is any answer to the question 'Why?'.

This is not the only way of defining an attribution, or perhaps not even the best definition. However, it is a definition we can use with acceptable consistency when trying to identify attributions within the context of normal everyday conversation. *An attribution is any answer to the question 'Why?'.*

Causes, links and outcomes: A model of an attribution

Attributions can help us to understand what causes people to behave in the way they do. Reducing attributions to their component parts is an important element in this process. This section examines these component parts in detail. As an example, we will use the attribution, 'I was tired so I went to bed early.'

In the last section we defined an attribution as 'any answer to the question "Why?"'. The example 'I was tired so I went to bed early' qualifies as an attribution. It answers the question 'Why did you go to bed early?'. The first thing to note is that an attribution can be broken down into at least two elements: an event or outcome, and some factor that we identify as the cause of that outcome. In our example, the event or outcome is going to bed early and the factor identified as causing the early night is tiredness. As we examine the causal belief, we will need to describe properties of both the cause element and the outcome element of the statement. Attributions also suggest some link between a cause and an outcome. Any description of the attribution will need to describe that link.

So, to summarise, an adequate description of an attribution should provide information about three elements:

(i)   the cause (**C**)
(ii)   the outcome (**O**)
(iii) the link between C and O (**L**)

Other features of attributions are also worth noting at this point. First, in the attribution about going to bed early, only one cause (being tired) is offered from a range of possible causes. The person might have said, 'I was tired, there was nothing to watch on the television and I had to be up at six, so I went to bed early.' In that statement, three different causal explanations are offered for the same outcome. Remember that even when someone gives only one cause for an outcome, he or she may believe it was not the only cause. The same is true of outcomes. A single factor like tiredness could be the cause of several eventualities. For example, 'I was tired, so I didn't go out, I went to bed early instead.' One cause (being tired) has been used to explain two outcomes (staying at home and going to bed early). Beliefs about causality can, and often do, involve multiple causes and multiple outcomes.

Second, a single attribution is often just one part of a longer sequence of causal beliefs. In sequences of attributions, an outcome in one attribution can become a cause in the next. For example, imagine the following snippet of conversation:

SALLY: '*Did you see the game last night?*'
TOM: '*No. I was tired so I went to bed early.*'

We could say there are two attributions here. The first is 'I was tired so I went to bed early'. Being tired is a cause, going to bed early is an outcome. The second is 'I missed the game because I went to bed early'. Going to bed early has changed from being an outcome of being tired to a cause of missing the match. These elements all have implications for describing causal beliefs that will become clear as we begin to tackle problems of coding the dimensions of attributions.

DEVELOPMENT OF ATTRIBUTIONAL DIMENSIONS

Having described briefly what attributions are, this next section looks at the variety of descriptions that we can apply to an attribution. We can describe solid objects using three dimensions: height, length and depth. We can also describe attributions using different dimensions. Each dimension provides information about different aspects of a causal belief. Rating an attribution on different dimensions enables us to make accurate predictions concerning how a belief about causality is likely to influence behaviour.

A common criticism of attributional research concerns the lack of consistency when it comes to defining the different dimensions of causal beliefs. As one reviewer concluded from his review of this issue of definitions, 'the measurement problem is one of terminological confusion compounded by psychometric imprecision'. To understand how and why differences have arisen, we will look at three key issues: the origins of different attributional dimensions, the purposes for which they were first defined, and how definitions have been adopted and adapted by successive attribution researchers.

The internal–external dimension

We recognise this as the first dimension to be identified in the historical development of attribution theory. Fritz Heider (1958), usually credited as the founding father of attribution theory, defined it originally. He was interested in what he termed *phenomenal causality*. The underlying principle of phenomenal causality is that people are motivated to see their world as predictable and thus controllable. If the world were a place in which physical events and social behaviour occurred completely at random, we would have no control over our lives. However, once we have identified the cause of some event, social or physical, we can predict the occurrence of that event. In this way life becomes more controllable. For example, knowing about the causal relationship between rain and cloud, can help us predict the weather to some extent. We can thus control whether we get wet. For this reason, we are motivated to go around attributing causes to the events we observe.

Heider divided causes into two categories. They could be impersonal features of the surrounding environment, *external* to any individual, as in the rain and clouds example. Alternatively, they could be personal features of someone's *internal* characteristics. To help make the distinction more straightforward, Heider introduced the idea of intentionality into the picture. Any action being observed, he claimed, could only be attributed to an internal cause if it could at the same time be assumed that the person being observed (the actor) intended to behave in that way. If the person was merely reacting to a particular set of circumstances, then we should assume that the cause was external.

Jones and Davis (1965) further developed Heider's principles in their 'theory of correspondent inferences'. The theory of correspondent inferences is concerned with the ways in which people come up with explanations for each other's behaviour. Attributing someone's behaviour to an internal cause is the same as attributing that person's behaviour to a disposition or personality characteristic. Making an external attribution involves identifying the cause of the observed behaviour as some aspect of the situation or environment. When deciding whether observed behaviour is due to a disposition of the actor or circumstances, Jones and Davis claimed that people calculate two formulae. The first concerns the number of unique consequences or non-common effects produced by an action. The second considers the social desirability of the outcome of the action. We can describe an action as having few non-common effects if the purpose of the action could be achieved equally as well by another action. When the number of non-common effects is low, and the social desirability of the outcome is also low, an internal attribution is more likely. If the number of non-common effects is high, and social desirability of the outcome is high, then an external attribution is more likely. For example, you observe a friend shouting at somebody. Why is your friend shouting? Do you make an internal or external attribution? First, consider the non-common effects involved. The person being spoken to will hear what your friend is saying whether he shouts or talks at normal volume. The effects of the action, getting a point across, are identical in both cases. Thus, the number of non-common effects is low. Second, consider social desirability. It is generally considered bad manners to shout. Thus, social desirability is low. With low non-common effects and low social desirability, you decide that your friend is shouting because he is short tempered (internal attribution). However, what would your decision be if you knew that the person being spoken to was hard of hearing? Here is a non-common effect. If your friend does not shout, the person will not hear him. Similarly, by not shouting, he will not achieve the desired outcome, getting the point across. Thus, social desirability is high. With high non-common effects and high social desirability, you decide that the situation demands that your friend must shout (external attribution). Note that Heider's notion of intentionality is not used in Jones and Davis's description of the internal–external distinction.

Another significant development came from Kelley (1973). In this formula, people look for three different types of information when deciding on attributing someone's behaviour to internal or external causes. First is consistency information. The question asked is, 'How often has this person behaved in this way in the past?', i.e. how consistent is this action with the person's history of actions? Second is distinctiveness information. 'How often has this person behaved in this way when the situation has been different?', i.e. how distinctive is this behaviour to this situation? Finally there is consensus information. 'Given the situation, how many other people would behave in the same way as the person being observed?', i.e. how many other people would do this sort of thing in these circumstances?

The answers to all three questions are then used to decide whether an attribution is internal or external. If we can say that we observed the behaviour only because that particular person was there to do it, then the attribution will be an internal one. If, on the other hand, we could say that any other person would have behaved in the same way, then we make an external attribution. So, according to this definition, an attribution is internal when the actor has a record of the behaviour, when these particular circumstances always elicit this reaction, and when no one else would be expected to behave in the same way.

Other authors have settled for a definition of the internal–external dimension based on an idea, commonly used in the legal profession, of the 'reasonable person'. If the hypothetical reasonable person would have behaved in the same way the actor did, then we cannot attribute the behaviour to any disposition or personality trait of the actor's. We define an attribution as internal only when we can say that the cause was 'an individual difference or personality variable.' If we decide that any reasonable person would have acted in the same way under the prevailing circumstances, then we make an external attribution.

The four definitions of the internal–external dimension reviewed so far appear to have a particular theme in common. Heider made the distinction according to impersonal (external) versus personal (internal) causal factors. Jones and Davis equated internal attributions with attributing causality to a disposition or personality characteristic and external attributions with situational factors. In Kelley's model, internal attributions are made only when an action is said to reflect the particular personality of the actor. Finally, we can define internal attributions as those applied to behaviour that reflects an individual difference or personality variable. The common theme is that we equate internal attributions with personal causal factors, personality traits or dispositions. If we can attribute an event to some impersonal or situational factor, a feature of the environment, then we rate it as external.

Although this internal–external distinction is quite clear so far, confusion has crept in as a result of similar terms being used in social learning theories of personality. According to social learning theory, we learn new behaviour only when two conditions are satisfied. First, we value the reward or reinforcement on offer for learning the new behaviour. Second, we believe that learning the behaviour will result in our receiving the reward or reinforcer. Those people with a general belief that they have control over the rewards they receive in life are said to have an internal locus of control. Those believing that chance, fate or the behaviour of other people is responsible for the reinforcers they receive have an external locus of control.

Martin Seligman subsequently took up this locus of control idea in the learned helplessness model of depression. Seligman and his colleagues began their work with animals. They noticed that dogs used in experiments where they had no control over reinforcers or rewards found it difficult to learn new tasks. For example, dogs were placed in a box from which they were unable to avoid a mild electric shock. After making some initial attempts to escape, the animals would simply give up and sit down. They then put the same dogs into a similar box from which there was an available escape route. When they applied mild shock again, the dogs did not attempt to move although an escape route was available. Seligman concluded that the dogs had learned from the first experiment that they were helpless in the face of the mild shocks. They then generalised this belief to the second situation. Having learned that they were helpless the dogs did not attempt to escape though their situation had changed. Learned helplessness had set in.

In extending this principle to human behaviour, Seligman proposed the learned helplessness model of depression. Depressives, the theory maintained, typically believe that they have little control over the important outcomes in their lives and so simply give up responding. This accounts for the negative outlook and lethargic behaviour that characterise depression. If people believe that nothing they do will make anything better, they give up doing anything. Seligman's theory was simply that depressives have an external locus of control while the rest of us have a more internal locus of control.

However, several observations concerning the behaviour of people experiencing depression conflicted with Seligman's interpretation. In particular, researchers noted that many depressives blame themselves for having failed in some sphere of their lives. In other words, they have an internal locus of control for these failures. Seligman and his team offered a reformulation of the learned helplessness theory of depression that incorporated the principles of attribution theory. This new version retained the internal–external dimension but gave it a new definition. Unlike previous formulations that, it was claimed, focus on whether a factor resides 'within the skin' or 'outside the skin', the new definition is related to the self-other dichotomy. When individuals believe that outcomes are either more or less likely to happen to themselves than to relevant others, we say that they attribute those outcomes to internal factors. On the other hand, if individuals believe that outcomes are as likely to happen to themselves as to relevant others, they are attributing them to external factors. Using this definition of the internal–external dimension enables us to make an important distinction between personal and universal helplessness. Reproduction of the table that Abramson and her colleagues used might help to clarify the issue (Figure 1.1).

		SELF	
		The person expects the outcome is contingent on a response in his or her repertoire	The person expects the outcome is not contingent on any response in his or her repertoire
OTHER	The person expects the outcome is contingent on a response in the repertoire of a relevant other	1	Personal helplessness 3 (internal attribution)
	The person expects the outcome is not contingent on a response in the repertoire of any relevant other	2	Universal helplessness 4 (external attribution)

Figure 1.1 The Internal–External dichotomy (from Abramson, Seligman & Teasdale, 1978)

Take this example of an attribution: 'I went to bed because I had a cold.' According to the definition above, that would be an external attribution because many people would go to bed in the same circumstances. The attribution does not reflect any personal or dispositional characteristic of the person whose behaviour is being explained. However, the cause in this attribution, a cold, is located within the person, so would be rated internal. A second example: 'I went to bed because my TV wouldn't work.' Here the attribution does suggest something personal or unique about the person. Most people do not take to their beds when their television breaks down. On this basis the attribution is rated internal. However, the cause of the behaviour, the TV malfunction, is located in the environment and so should be rated external.

Confusion has arisen over the internal–external dimension partly because the term has been used both by Heider in his work on phenomenal causality, and by Rotter's social learning theory. The extreme popularity of the learned helplessness paradigm, which has used both definitions of the internal–external dimension at different stages in its development, has served to add to the confusion.

The authors have attempted to reconcile this problem by using two distinct dimensions, internal–external and personal–universal. The internal–external dimension is coded according to the locus of the cause element in an attribution. The personal–universal dimension concerns whether something unique about an individual is implied in an attribution. It is coded by looking not just at the cause element of an attribution, but at all three elements, cause, link and outcome. An attribution with a cause coded internal may or may not contain information concerning a unique characteristic of an individual.

The stable–unstable dimension

Mercifully, the historical background to this dimension is much less complex than that surrounding the internal–external dimension. It originates from Weiner's attributional theory of achievement motivation, based on an original idea from Atkinson. Atkinson claimed that people are motivated to engage in tasks according to how proud they are of their achievements. If they have experienced failure at similar tasks in the past, or attribute their success to how easy the task was, then they are less likely to have this sense of pride. Without the pride there is less motivation to engage in other similar activity.

Weiner added an attributional component to this idea by saying that personal responsibility for achievement or failure influenced motivation. People high on achievement motivation often attribute success to ability and effort, and failure to lack of effort. On the other hand, people low on achievement motivation tend to attribute success to luck or other external factors, and failure to lack of ability.

The stable–unstable dimension is used to predict the extent to which people will expect to be successful in future tasks. This expectancy, says Weiner, depends on whether outcomes have been attributed to stable or unstable causes. Attributing success to stable or persistent causes will lead to high expectancy of future success. Similarly, attributing failure to unstable or transient causes also maintains expectancy of future success. For example, take motivation to work hard at academic study. Passing an examination could be attributed to intelligence or the possibility that it was just an easy exam. Intelligence is a relatively stable factor. Passing this exam because of one's intelligence would tend to make one optimistic about exam success in the future, and motivate one to continue working hard. Failing the exam, but attributing failure to some external cause, such as it was just an unreasonably difficult paper, would not necessarily make one any less optimistic of exam success in the future.

Attributing success to unstable or transient causes and failure to stable causes will have the reverse impact on expectancies. If we attribute an exam failure to stupidity, we are likely to be pessimistic when it comes to subsequent exams, and thus not too motivated to work hard. If we had attributed success to an unstable or transient cause such as it being an uncommonly easy exam, there would also be scant grounds for future optimism.

The global–specific dimension

The global–specific dimension was developed as part of the reformulated learned helplessness model of depression. A belief that one is helpless can be very specific to a particular area of our lives. Alternatively, we might generalise helplessness to all aspects of our lives. Having experienced failure in one specific arena, depressives will typically develop a generalised belief that everything they do will fail. Causes rated as global are those that are likely to have an impact on a wide range of different situations. Those rated as specific will only influence a small range of situations.

The controllable–uncontrollable dimension

The controllable–uncontrollable dimension is very much rooted in the locus of control idea discussed earlier. It was incorporated into the attributional literature by Weiner in his achievement motivation model. According to Weiner, attributions concerning control have some influence over emotional reactions to success or failure. For example, where people believe they had control over some negative outcome they experienced, they are more likely to experience feelings of guilt. I am more likely to feel guilty about failing my examination if I believe I could have passed had I tried.

The only source of controversy surrounding this dimension concerns which of the three elements of an attribution—cause, link or outcome—we rate for control. In the attribution 'I went to bed because I had a cold', the speaker definitely has control over the outcome element, going to bed. However, the speaker may believe that he or she had no control over the cause, having a cold. Is the attribution rated controllable or uncontrollable? Many similar examples are to be found when looking for attributions in normal conversation.

This section has looked at the historical development of attribution theory and the ways in which dimensions have evolved. The process of evolution is not over. We have developed working definitions based on our own research work. These are not the only definitions in current use, and without doubt will not be the last. Definitions may change according to the context in which attributional research takes place. However, to evaluate research, some move towards standardisation seems desirable.

DEFINING THE DIMENSIONS OF ATTRIBUTIONS

As we have discussed, not all attribution researchers use the same dimensions to describe causal beliefs. Even when we give the dimensions used the same names, definitions of each can differ from study to study. This is a problem when it comes to evaluating findings. The authors have carried out detailed examinations of the different dimensions and definitions that people have used in attribution research. In the interests of consistency, we proposed five dimensions broadly representative of the diverse collection found in the literature. To show how each of the five dimensions is applied to an attribution, think about the following example:

I failed the exam because I'm stupid

This is evidently an attribution, because it answers the question '*why* did you fail the exam?'. The speaker's lack of intellectual ability caused the event, failing the exam. We can now categorise this statement according to our five dimensions. Each dimension is bipolar, meaning that it has two extremes.

First is the *stable–unstable* dimension. To rate on this dimension involves looking at the cause element of the attribution. If the speaker believes that the cause is something unlikely to change in the future, then we rate the attribution as stable. If the event occurred because of some temporary state of affairs, the cause is rated unstable. In the example being used here, the cause of exam failure is clearly a long-term condition. Being stupid is a factor that is unlikely to change. Therefore, we would rate the attribution as stable on this dimension. On the other hand, if the attribution had been 'I failed the exam because I was tired', the rating would have been unstable. Tiredness is more of a temporary condition than stupidity.

The second is the *global–specific* dimension. It concerns the cause element of the attribution again. Rating on this dimension reflects the extent to which someone believes that a cause will influence outcomes other than the one identified in the attribution. In the exam failure example, the cause of failure was stupidity. Stupidity is likely to affect events other than just exams. For example, getting a job or gaining admission to a postgraduate training course. We categorise causes that can affect other outcomes as global. Had the attribution been 'I failed the exam because I was tired', the cause would probably be rated specific. Being tired on this particular day is unlikely to have important effects on a wide range of other outcomes.

Third is the *internal–external* dimension. Applied also to the cause element of the attribution, the internal–external dimension concerns the origins of a cause. Internal causes come from within the person. External causes are found in the person's surrounding environment. In the example of exam failure, stupidity is something that comes from within the person. We would rate this attribution as internal. If the cause had been the weather, 'I failed the exam because it was too hot to think', the attribution would have been rated external. Had the cause been somebody else's behaviour, 'I failed the exam because my roommate locked me in the bathroom', the rating would be external again.

Fourth is the *personal–universal* dimension. Rating on this dimension depends on whether any elements of the attribution, cause outcome or link, tells us anything particular, or personal, about the speaker. The example attribution provides information about the speaker's intellectual abilities and so would be rated personal. In the causal statement, 'I failed the exam because it was very difficult', the implication is that most people would have failed given the circumstances. This attribution, because it tells us nothing unique about the speaker, would be rated universal.

Fifth is the *controllable–uncontrollable* dimension. We apply it to all elements of an attribution. If the speaker feels that he or she could have had some influence over the link, the cause or the outcome, the attribution is rated controllable. Failing an exam due to stupidity is something that most people would consider being outside their control. Here the attribution would be rated uncontrollable. What if the attribution had been 'I failed the exam because I got very drunk the night before'? Here we might assume that the speaker could have chosen not to go out drinking. He or she could have exercised some element of control. The attribution would be rated controllable.

To summarise this section on the dimensions of attributions, we can take a final look at our example 'I failed the exam because I'm stupid'. Table 1.1 summarises ratings for this attribution, and provides the rationale for the rating on each dimension.

TABLE 1.1   Attributional codings

Rating	Rationale
Stable	Stupidity is something that cannot be changed in a short time.
Global	Being stupid is likely to have an effect on other outcomes, not just failing the exam.
Internal	Stupidity is a feature of the person speaking, not a feature of the situation.
Personal	The attribution tells us something particular or unique about the person speaking, that he or she is stupid.
Uncontrollable	Given that the speaker is stupid, there is nothing he or she could have done about failing the exam.

THE PRACTICAL APPLICATION OF ATTRIBUTIONAL APPROACHES

The purpose of this book is not just to introduce the reader to the principles of attribution theory. What makes the investigation of causal beliefs so interesting is that it has considerable practical applications. In this section, we will discuss three studies that have used an attributional approach. In each case, results of the study have practical implications. These particular studies have been chosen because they are broadly representative of applied research using attribution theory.

Investigating ADD and hyperactive behaviour

The first looks at the treatment of Attention Deficit Disorder (ADD) in children (Borden & Brown, 1989). ADD is more commonly diagnosed in the USA than in the UK. Symptoms include a lack of ability to concentrate or hold attention, along with, in some cases, hyperactive behaviour.

A common method of treating ADD is through stimulant drugs. However, there are drawbacks to the use of medication in these circumstances. Prescribing drugs can encourage a belief in patients and their families that the problem behaviour is something over which they have no control.

The attributional dimension of interest in this instance is the one labelled controllable–uncontrollable. Patients who believe they do not have any control over their symptoms are often less compliant with treatment regimes. For example, those who believe that they have no control over their body weight are less likely to keep to dietary or exercise programmes. Poorly motivated patients are less likely to take an active role in their treatment.

The study addresses two questions. Are treatments involving medication associated with parents and children believing that they have no control over possible solutions to the problem of ADD? Similarly: Does treatment involving cognitive therapy alone lead to more controllable attributions being made?

They divided 30 children, at random, into three treatment groups. Group A had only cognitive therapy. They gave group B cognitive therapy plus methylphenidate (a stimulant drug). They gave group C cognitive therapy plus a placebo. Following each of the treatment programmes, they asked parents and children to make attributions for the cause of, and possible solutions to, the problem of ADD.

Results showed that attributions concerning possible solutions made by parents were different depending on which of the three treatment groups their children were in. Parents whose children had been in group A, no medication, were most likely to think that their children could solve the ADD problem through their own efforts. Parents whose children had been in group C, cognitive therapy plus placebo, were the least likely to adopt the same view. Parents' attributions for the cause of ADD did not differ across the three treatment groups. Children's attributions for either the cause and the solution to the ADD problem did not show any differences as a result of being in different treatment groups.

Generally, results suggested that the more parents believed that medication was the solution to ADD, the worse was their rating of their child's behaviour.

The authors of the study concluded that there was some support for the view that different treatments are responsible for bringing about different attributions. Parents of children who received only cognitive therapy (group A) were more likely than those receiving cognitive therapy and placebo (group C) to believe that solutions to the ADD problem were controllable.

The study showed how consideration of attributions is important when planning treatment programmes. Different types of treatment can encourage different kinds of causal beliefs in patients. These causal beliefs can have effects on behaviour, particularly when it comes to taking responsibility for one's own health.

Of course these conclusions are not only applicable to the treatment of ADD; they apply to the treatment of any condition where clinicians give medication. The treatment of the depressive disorders is a case in point. Antidepressant medication is often given as a short-term respite measure. Treatment for depression also often involves cognitive therapy, some of which will emphasise the need to take responsibility for and control over events. If patients believe that medication, not their own efforts, causes improvements, they are less likely to assume control and manage their own difficulties. On the contrary, it is this belief in medication as a solution that can often create the ideal conditions for the onset of addiction.

This study has shown how analysis of attributions in a medical context has led to the development of some practical advice. This advice is relevant to any clinical situation in which we require effective treatment programmes.

Motivations in graduate job search

The second study examined the attitudes and behaviours of students looking for work following graduation (Kulik & Rowland, 1989). The study was interested in factors influencing the extent to which students get actively involved in the search for a job. They looked at three dimensions of attributions. First, the

internal–external dimension. From the brief definitions discussed earlier, you may remember that internal attributions include ability or effort, while external attributions include luck or
task difficulty. Second is the stable–unstable dimension. Stable
causes can include mental ability, while an example of an unstable cause might be tiredness. One is relatively permanent, the
other temporary. Third is the controllable–uncontrollable
dimension. In this study they defined the dimension as 'the
amount of control the individual has over the causal factors'.
They gave examples in which they described effort as controllable and ability as uncontrollable.

The study set out to answer two questions:

1. Do people who think of themselves as successful in looking
   for jobs have different attributions to those who see themselves as unsuccessful?
2. Do those people who put more effort into the search for
   work have different attributions than those who get less
   actively involved?

A small sample of 20 undergraduates enrolled in an American
business school took part. The students were searching for a job
to take up after their graduation. They were asked to make
attributions concerning their efforts the beginning, the middle
and the end of their search for a job.

Results showed that different groups of students changed
their causal beliefs over the period during which they participated in the study. Students who ultimately failed to find a job
had made stable and internal causes for their anticipated outcomes at the beginning of the study. However, as time went on,
they rated the impact of stable and internal causes as progres-
sively less important. Students who were successful also provided causal explanations that were stable and internal at the
beginning of the study. However, the difference was that they
maintained this pattern consistently throughout their search for
work.

People less actively involved in looking for a job rated unstable factors as highly important at the beginning of the study,
but as much less important by the end. In contrast, those people
who maintained a high level of active searching throughout the

study rated unstable casual factors as highly important throughout the study.

What do these results mean in terms of the two research questions? First, do those who think of themselves as successful in looking for jobs have different attributions to those who see themselves as less successful? Students rating themselves as successful maintained a belief that stable and internal factors were important for those outcomes. The people who felt that their efforts ultimately resulted in failure put less emphasis on stable, internal factors as time went on. This result is generally consistent with similar research. People often attribute failure to less internal and stable causes to maintain their self-esteem. For example, being turned down for a job due to lack of intelligence (a stable, internal cause) is likely to make people feel quite negatively about themselves. On the other hand, putting failure down to a relative of the boss getting the job (an unstable, external cause) is less likely to induce negative self-esteem. People who put less emphasis on the importance of stable internal factors retain an optimistic view and so protect their self-esteem.

The second research question was whether those who put more effort into the search for work have different attributions than those less actively involved. Those more actively involved in searching for work were more likely to believe that unstable factors were important in determining success. By attributing success to unstable factors we can believe that there is always a chance of success. For example, if I believe that I am an unlucky person (stable attribution) I will not gamble. If I believe that the winning is down to chance (unstable attribution) I may be more likely to gamble. To summarise, if people believe in the potential for change, they are more likely to maintain a high degree of effort.

The study has practical implications for those working in the careers advice field. Changing people's attributions for success and failure in finding work can affect both their behavioural and emotional reactions. Encouraging a belief in internal factors, like ability and effort, can encourage people to be more satisfied with the outcome if that outcome is successful. However, if they attribute failure to find work to the same internal causes, it may lead to a loss of self-esteem and lack of motivation to continue the search. Career counsellors also need to emphasise unstable factors when it comes to explaining the reasons for failure to get a particular job. This can encourage the individual to keep looking for new opportunities. This relationship between attributions and motivation has practical implications for any domain in which performance is important. Sports psychology, occupational psychology and health psychology are just three areas that spring to mind.

Attributions and health

The third study in this illustrative sample is concerned with health promotion (Quadrel & Lau, 1989). The aim is to examine the effects that promotions designed to provide information about health care have on people's health knowledge and health-related behaviour. Attribution theory has been used in this context to develop what we know as the Health Care Belief Model (HCBM). According to this model, people will only adopt healthy behaviour if they: (a) put a high value on good health, and (b) believe that they can exercise control over their own health.

The study examined whether attributions on the controllable–uncontrollable dimension influenced responses to health promotions. If people believe that good health is largely uncontrollable, will they respond better to health promotions that reflect this belief. Similarly, will those who believe they do have some control over their own health respond more favourably to promotions that reinforce this control aspect of health care?

The study was in two parts. The first looked at whether people who put a high value on, and believed that they could exercise control over, their own health were more likely to look for and take notice of information about health care. The second part was concerned with beliefs about control and how they influence the extent to which people take notice of health promotions. Would the kind of message being put across in promotions interact with people's existing beliefs about health? Would that interaction affect behaviour?

The study was part of a larger investigation that followed more than 1,000 students through their three-year college career. In part one, they divided students into two groups. They gave group 1 a booklet containing information about health and fitness. Group 2 received no booklet, but received an invitation to attend an exhibition concerning health issues. The hypothesis was that students who placed a high value on physical health, believed that their health was controllable and received the health booklet would score highest on subsequent tests of health knowledge. Because women feel more responsible for their health than men, they also included gender as a factor in the experimental design.

They asked that all participants complete questionnaires about their health control beliefs and the extent to which they place a high value on their health. In addition, everybody completed a test of health knowledge. Results confirmed the suspected sex differences in health care beliefs. Women who scored high on health value and high on control but who did not receive the health and fitness booklet scored higher on the test of health knowledge than men with high health value and high control who did not get copies of the booklet. Men with high health value and high control who received the booklet scored highest on the health knowledge test. Results suggest that men are most likely to benefit from the kind of health care promotion that relies on the provision of information. Women, at least those who go to college, already possess quite a high degree of information concerning their own health.

The second part of the study involved two groups of women only. They gave each group one of two alternative messages promoting a breast self-examination workshop. One message, entitled 'Control Breast Cancer' laid great emphasis on the ability of women to take control over their health by doing regular self-examination. The second message, 'Don't Press Your Luck', placed the greater emphasis on the part played by luck in the development of breast cancer. It explained that breast cancer strikes in a relatively random fashion, and that the most effective treatment depends on early detection.

Again they assessed the value that subjects placed on their health and their beliefs concerning health control through questionnaires. During the term that followed receipt of the different messages, they asked students about the frequency with which they examined their breasts.

Women who placed a high value on health and were high on health control beliefs showed the most improvement in their self-examination behaviour after receiving the messages. The most dramatic improvements were evident when there was consistency between the type of message the women received (control vs chance) and their own beliefs concerning the controllability of health outcomes. Those women who believed more in chance health outcomes responded best to the message emphasising chance as a factor in breast cancer. Similarly, those believing in health control responded best to the control message. People with different control beliefs responded differently to health promotions depending on the underlying emphasis of the message.

Overall, these two studies show that people differ considerably concerning beliefs about control over health. Furthermore, this makes a difference in the way in which people respond to campaigns aimed to promote health issues. The first part of the study showed that individuals with high control beliefs are more likely to take notice of information concerning health. This is especially true for men. The second part showed that the use of different techniques to put across a health message can influence behaviour depending on people's existing beliefs about their own health.

Two practical implications can be drawn from the study. First, health education needs to address the issue of public awareness concerning the value of good health. Health promotion should emphasise the ability of people to take control over their own health through adopting illness-preventative behaviours. Second, carefully targeting different kinds of messages could make health promotion campaigns more effective. For groups high on health value and control, information needs to be presented in a way that is consistent with those beliefs. The same is true for those low on control beliefs. Before we formulate health promotion messages, we need to consider the beliefs of the target group at whom we are aiming the message.

Results from this study are equally applicable to other types of promotion campaigns. Consumers of health care are consumers in the same way as people who buy food products, motor cars or electrical goods. A campaign promoting safety aspects of a car will be ineffective if the target audience believes that surviving accidents is a matter of chance. Similarly, promoting health aspects of a low-fat spread would only succeed if we convinced buyers that diet determines heart disease.

CONCLUSIONS

In this chapter, we have explained how attribution theory relates to behavioural and cognitive theories of learning, what attributions are, and how attribution theory has been applied to practical problems. The great strength of research based on analysis of causal beliefs is not only the strong theory in which it is grounded but also, as we hope to have shown, its practical utility. The next chapter will introduce a particular method of identifying and coding attributions developed and subsequently used by the authors.

2

Coding attributions

This chapter aims to describe a method of coding attributions known as the Leeds Attributional Coding System, or LACS for short. The system was developed by a group of researchers and clinicians working in the Leeds Family Therapy and Research Centre (LFTRC). The group were interested in how attribution theory might help therapists to understand complex family beliefs about the causes of their difficulties. Existing methods of exploring causal beliefs appeared too crude. It had been assumed that attributions were private cognitions that required questionnaires, behavioural vignettes, or hypothetical laboratory simulations to render them open to investigation. The LFTRC team set out to devise a method of coding attributions that could be applied to real causal beliefs expressed during family therapy sessions (Stratton *et al.*, 1988).

Using the LACS allows qualitative material to be quantified in a way that makes statistical analysis possible. Alternatively, the method can be used to look systematically at the content of attributions, exploring the unique way in which individuals explain different events. Under examination are what we call 'public attributions', that is causal beliefs expressed in conversation or in writing. Examples of situations in which public attributions are made include clinical interviews, letters, speeches, focus groups or publicity materials. In this chapter we use material from research into candidates' impression management during selection interviews to illustrate how the LACS works.

BACKGROUND TO ATTRIBUTIONAL CODING

Attribution theory concerns the everyday causal explanations that people produce when they encounter novel, important, unusual or potentially threatening behaviour and events. According to attribution theorists, people are motivated to identify the causes of such events, because by doing so they render their environment more predictable and potentially more controllable.

Particular attention has been paid by attribution researchers to individual differences in the way people typically explain outcomes. Such differences are known generally as 'attributional style' and are seen by many psychologists as representing a cognitive personality trait. The most common means for exploring attributional style has been the questionnaire. Two of the best-known examples are the Attributional Style Questionnaire, or ASQ, developed by Martin Seligman and his colleagues (Schulman, Castellon & Seligman, 1989), and the Occupational Attributional Style Questionnaire, OASQ, developed by Adrian Furnham (Furnham, Sadka & Brewin, 1992). Both questionnaires ask respondents to think about hypothetical positive events (e.g. *you secured the promotion you were looking for*) and hypothetical negative events (e.g. *your presentation went badly*), identify a possible cause for each event and then rate that cause on several dimensions. Another popular approach has been to use behavioural vignettes describing an event. Respondents are asked to make a guess as to possible causes of the hypothetical event. Similarly, role-play situations have required people to rate possible causes for their own and their partner's behaviour along several causal dimensions.

From a research perspective, using laboratory methods to tap causal beliefs has obvious advantages. Questionnaires and vignettes are easy to administer, the results are instantly quantifiable, and respondents all rate the same events. However, laboratory methods also have important limitations. For example, hypothetical events focus attention on issues that the investigator rather than the respondent may consider meaningful or important. Events are frequently presented as isolated incidents; additional contextual information often provided during normal conversation is lost. Finally, the respondent has almost no opportunity to negotiate the meaning or relevance of an attribution with the investigator.

Talking about causal beliefs is a social, not just a private, phenomenon. People are not only motivated to make sense of their world for their own private understanding; they need to share their understanding to interact successfully with others. Individuals negotiate a shared reality through conversation that enables them to understand the causes of events from the perspective of others. The social nature of attributions means that we need to pay more attention to causal beliefs expressed spontaneously during conversation. Many of our beliefs about causality are adopted second hand through social interaction. The prevalence and importance of social attributions is likely to be appreciated by anyone who has taken part in gossip, whether it is among friends, at work or even within our own families.

Attributions occur regularly and frequently in everyday conversation, particularly when people discuss events that are unusual, important and mutually relevant. Consequently, several social contexts are being opened up to attributional analysis. In the context of work, the range has included team meetings and appraisal situations, interpersonal decisions in selection interviews, exchanges with customers and even letters to shareholders presented in organisations' annual reports.

DESCRIPTION OF THE LACS METHOD

This section focuses on the Leeds Attributional Coding System (LACS), a system that benefits from having an extensive coding framework. The LACS is also unusual in that it enables us to explore attributions made by one person, which concern the behaviour or actions of other people. Since first developed some 10 years ago, the system has been used in a variety of clinical and non-clinical settings.

Many examples used in this section are taken from research into causal beliefs expressed during job interviews. A particular study is described in more detail in Chapter 4. The data described here come from graduate recruitment interviews carried out by a multinational oil company. The purpose of the research was to follow up an earlier investigation concerning the types of attributions made by successful and unsuccessful candidates during selection interviews. Results suggested that candidates making more stable, personal and controllable attributions for negative outcomes attributions were more likely to be rated favourably by interviewers.

The selection interview is arguably an ideal situation for exploring public attributions. Candidates enter interviews assuming that they have to justify why they are suited to the job. Interviewers frequently ask candidates why they have applied to work for their company. The implicit belief is that answers can be used to predict how the candidate might react in future work situations.

Before you start

The system is concerned with quantifying qualitative data. Using the LACS, attributions taken from written or spoken materials are transformed or coded into numbers to make them more amenable to statistical analysis. Attributions can be identified, coded and counted. To help with the analysis stage of the process, we have devised a coding frame that may be useful. The frame offers a method of recording the numbers generated from the coding of each attribution. The design of the frame reflects our use of the Statistical Package for the Social Sciences (SPSS) to analyse much of our data. Evidently other software packages can do the same job. Other coding frames can be designed quite easily for use with alternative packages.

A word of caution before we explain the workings of the LACS in more detail. At each stage of the process, the researcher is required to make subjective judgements. For example, questions will arise such as 'Is this statement an attribution?' or 'Is the attribution coded as controllable or uncontrollable?'. To make subjective judgements as consistent as possible, we have tried to provide definitions and descriptions that are unambiguous. However, it is inevitable that some attributions do not fall neatly into one category or another. We speak from experience when we say that these examples can be the most frustrating. If problems occur with some aspects of the coding process, check your understanding of the definitions concerned. One solution may be to drop ambiguous examples from your analysis. Alternatively, it may help to ask someone else to try to code difficult material just to check that your judgements are as consistent as possible. We will come back to this issue of reliability later in the chapter. For the moment, remember that this is not an exercise in precise measurement. As yet, we have no totally reliable ways of measuring what people think (thankfully).

Finally, before starting your attributional analysis, think very carefully about how your investigation is informed by theory. Kurt Lewin, a social psychologist, once famously remarked that 'there is nothing so practical as a good theory'. Theory tells us what kind of data we should be collecting. Before coding your attributions on all of the dimensions we describe, in the hope that something interesting may appear, think again. Your investigation should be driven by theory. A careful choice may make it unlikely that all the dimensions will need coding. For example, several theories of human behaviour concentrate on the internal–external dimension, while others make specific hypotheses concerning the controllable–uncontrollable dimension. It is generally poor science to collect masses of data and then embark on a fishing trip in search of random patterns, the significance of which one then tries to interpret.

The six stages of attributional coding as defined by the LACS

Figure 2.1 illustrates the six stages involved in coding attributions.

1. Identify sources of attributions

Coding focuses on public attributions extracted either from transcripts of discourse or from material already in written form. Any discourse that can be audiotaped and transcribed can be used as a potential source of attributions. Examples reported in research include clinical interviews, speeches, team meetings,

```
┌─────────────────────────────────────────────────────────────────┐
│  1. Identify source of attributions                              │
└─────────────────────────────────────────────────────────────────┘

┌─────────────────────────────────────────────────────────────────┐
│  2. Extract attributions                                         │
└─────────────────────────────────────────────────────────────────┘

┌─────────────────────────────────────────────────────────────────┐
│  3. Separate cause and outcome elements of the attribution       │
└─────────────────────────────────────────────────────────────────┘

┌─────────────────────────────────────────────────────────────────┐
│  4. Identify Speaker, Agent and Target                           │
└─────────────────────────────────────────────────────────────────┘

┌─────────────────────────────────────────────────────────────────┐
│  5. Code attributions on causal dimensions:                      │
│        Stable–Unstable                                           │
│        Global–Specific                                           │
│        Internal–External                                         │
│        Personal–Universal                                        │
│        Controllable–Uncontrollable                               │
└─────────────────────────────────────────────────────────────────┘

┌─────────────────────────────────────────────────────────────────┐
│  6. Analysis                                                     │
└─────────────────────────────────────────────────────────────────┘
```

Figure 2.1   Stages of attributional coding

semi-structured research interviews, or written archival material such as annual reports or letters to shareholders. However, while attributions are usually present in most types of material, certain sources may not be as rich as others. Technical descriptions or interviews concerned with factual or problem-solving issues often generate fewer attributions than discussions of important events or justifications of decisions and behaviour. Typically, semi-structured research interviews will generate approximately 1–2 attributions per minute. In research used to illustrate this section, candidates produced between 40 and 100 attributional statements during 30-minute selection interviews.

Negotiating permission to audiotape interviews or other discourse material is essential, as permission is likely to depend on the sensitivity of the material being recorded. The selection interview is just one example of a situation in which it would be unethical to audiotape unless permission has been obtained from candidates in advance.

2. Extract attributions

Different researchers have used different definitions of an attribution. In the previous chapter, an attribution was defined as 'any answer to the question "why?"'. Another research group, studying spontaneous attributions produced by survivors of the *Herald of Free Enterprise* disaster, used a different approach (Joseph, Brewin, Yule & Williams, 1993). They defined causal attributions as 'Statements identifying a factor or factors that contribute to a given outcome' where 'a stated or implied causal relationship has to be present'. The research team that developed the LACS have defined an attribution as 'Any statement in which an outcome is indicated as having happened, or being present, because of some identified event or condition'. The important thing it not so much which definition of an attribution is used, but that the chosen definition is used consistently throughout the extraction process.

This stage of the process involves pulling out attributions from your qualitative data. Some experienced researchers have identified and extracted attributions from simply listening to taped interviews. However, for the inexperienced, this can lead to a reduction in reliability, and difficulties for coders who may lack additional contextual information available in a transcript. While recognising the time and effort involved, we would recommend that those unfamiliar with the process try to generate verbatim transcripts of the discourse they intend to use.

It takes a little practice to identify attributions quickly and reliably. Some attributions are more obvious than others and many will include a causal connective such as 'because', 'so', 'therefore', 'as a result'. Nevertheless, in some attributions a causal relationship is implied rather than stated explicitly. For example, take the case of *'He's never liked dogs, he was bitten when he was young'*. In this attribution no link word appears, although the speaker clearly believes that being bitten has caused the person described in the statement to dislike dogs. In interviews, one can often explicitly request a causal explanation. For example, a job interviewer might ask *'Why do you want this job?'*. Similarly, although speakers do generate simple causal statements (e.g. *I will get selected for the tennis team if the teacher likes me*), often causal statements are complex and may be best described as a causal sequence. This is illustrated in the following example:

INTERVIEWER: *Can you give me an example of a target where you weren't successful?*

CANDIDATE: *OK, well I think the biggest target I didn't achieve was my undergraduate degree and that was possibly my biggest disappointment. Maybe that was one area where I didn't sort of impose the target well, you know. I didn't realise or make myself achieve that target. Maybe I didn't plan that as well as I should have done and I think, you know, that is certainly the biggest target that I didn't achieve, you know, in the long run.*

INTERVIEWER: *So what do you think were the causes of that failure?*

CANDIDATE: *I think, I think there are several. I think there are a combination of reasons for that particular failure to reach that target. It was some aspects of the course which were not really focused in an applied way. Some aspects of the geology were very fringe geology and I was more interested in the physics, geophysics side of things. So there was that aspect. I think a very serious problem was that I was more focused on aspects that I was interested in rather than focusing on the target of achieving the examination, which I knew I should have got. And looking back that was certainly a problem in the first and second years. I was concentrating on areas that I was more interested in rather than on aspects that I needed to concentrate on to pass the exam.*

INTERVIEWER: *Right.*

CANDIDATE: *So those are probably the two reasons that I would attribute to not reaching that particular target.*

INTERVIEWER: *OK. How did you deal with that failure or what you regard as failure, I mean, I mean what degree did you finally get?*

CANDIDATE: *I got a 2:2.*

Although the interviewer was not aware that the researcher was interested in causal attributions, he requests specific causes of the candidate in this excerpt. The response provided by the candidate also illustrates the fact that people do not generally think in terms of simple cause and effect relationships. In this example several causes are provided. Consequently, we recommend extracting and coding each attribution separately. Some researchers have chosen to extract causal paragraphs rather than causal sentences, and while this can make extracting attributions easier, it does pose difficulties for later coding.

3. Separate cause and outcome elements of the attribution

The previous chapter described two specific elements of an attribution: a cause and an outcome. Because different dimensions in the LACS are applied to either the cause or the outcome elements of an attribution, distinguishing between the two before coding starts is useful. In the previous example, the speaker provides several different, even contradictory causes for the same outcome. The LACS suggests that in such cases the researcher should identify the outcome (e.g. failing in a test) and then list each of the stated causes separately (e.g. *not being good at mathematics, not revising enough, a poor lecturer*). These are treated as separate causal statements for later coding. When identifying causal attributions in transcripts, distinguishing between causes and outcomes is useful. A common convention is to underline a cause, insert an arrow (←) pointing in the direction of the outcome, and a '/' showing approximately where the outcome ends (when an outcome follows a cause) or begins (when the outcome precedes a cause). This is shown in the following example:

INTERVIEWER: *Can you give me an example of a target where you weren't successful?*

CANDIDATE: *OK, well I think / the biggest target I didn't achieve was my undergraduate degree (and that was possibly my biggest disappointment. Maybe that was one area where)* (1) ←* I didn't

---

*Note that in this extract brackets have been placed around the text here because it separates a cause and an outcome and would not be included as part of the extracted causal attribution.

sort of impose the target well, you know. (2) ← I didn't realise or make myself achieve that target. (3) ← Maybe I didn't plan that as well as I should have done, and I think, you know, that is certainly the biggest target that I didn't achieve, you know, in the long run.

INTERVIEWER: *So what do you think were the causes of / that failure?*

CANDIDATE: *I think, I think there are several, I think there are a combination of reasons for that particular failure to reach that target. (4) ← It was some aspects of the course which were not really focused in an applied way. (5) ← Some aspects of the geology were very fringe geology and (6) ← I was more interested in the physics, geophysics side of things. So there was that aspect. I think a very serious problem was that (7) ← I was more focused on aspects that I was interested in rather than focusing on the target of achieving the examination, which I knew I should have got. And looking back that was certainly a problem in the first and second years. (8) ← I was concentrating on areas that I was more interested in rather than on aspects that I needed to concentrate on to pass the exam.*

INTERVIEWER: *Right.*

CANDIDATE: *So those are probably the two reasons that I would attribute to not reaching that particular target.*

INTERVIEWER: *OK. How did you deal with that failure or what you regard as failure, I mean, I mean what degree did you finally get?*

CANDIDATE: *I got a 2:2.*

It is probably worth restating at this point that extracting and coding attributions is not something that one might describe as

---

Here the interviewer provides an outcome in the form of a question that would be extracted as '*I failed in this target (getting a good grade) because . . .*' and the individual causes would be extracted and listed as:

(1)   ← *I didn't sort of impose the target well.*
(2)   ← *I didn't realise or make myself achieve that target.*
(3)   ← *Maybe I didn't plan that as well as I should have done.*
(4)   ← *It was some aspects of the course which were not really focused in an applied way.*
(5)   ← *Some aspects of the geology were very fringe geology.*
(6)   ← *I was more interested in the physics, geophysics side of things.*
(7)   ← *I was more focused on aspects that I was interested in rather than focusing on the target of achieving the examination.*
(8)   ← *I was concentrating on areas that I was more interested in rather than on aspects that I needed to concentrate on to pass the exam.*

Although the last two causes appear to be very similar, the convention has been followed that all attributions are extracted, even if they are repeated.

an 'exact science'. The beginning and end of an attribution are not always definite and it is worth remembering when extracting that attributions should make sense when isolated from the text.

Have a look at the following paragraphs of text and try to identify all the attributions. The text is an extract from an interview with the mother of a 5-year-old girl. The interview was conducted as part of a study investigating parents' attributions for their children's behaviour (Silvester, 1989). As part of 45-minute interviews, each mother was asked to describe situations when they were dissatisfied with their child's behaviour. At the end of the chapter are the results of our efforts to do the same job (Example 1). As a rough guide, keep practising until your ratings agree with ours in around 80% of extractions.

If you smack Karen, that just makes the problem worse. When she's naughty she'll defy you all the way and she won't give in. And if you smack her, because you've had enough of her defying you and telling you like, she'll say 'I don't love you, I'm going to run away'. Well all kids say things like that, so you take them in your stride. But if she carries on to the extent that you have to give her a smack 'cos she's really getting defiant here, she'll sit and scream and carry on and things like that. She'll throw herself into a tantrum so much that you feel like strangling her. But you don't strangle her, you have to give her a cuddle because she can't understand that when she's naughty and you're upset you can't cuddle her.

'Cos I put her into bed once with her being misbehaved and I couldn't do it no more 'cos she wrecked the bedroom. She threw everything on the floor, she tore all the wall paper off the wall, kicked the door and screamed. And all I could do was hear her screaming and carrying on. And it made me feel like going up and really smacking her hard. So now I can't do that.

See the Appendix at the end of this chapter for the extracted attributions from this passage.

Having extracted attributions from a transcript, the process of coding begins. If using computer software to analyse coded data, such as SPSS, systematically recording codings at the same time may help with later data entry. A coding template like the one illustrated in Figure 2.2 can be useful.

		1	2	3	4	5	6	7	8	9	10
1. Attribution number											
2. Speaker											
3. Agent											
4. Target											
5. Stable (1), Unstable (0)											
6. Global (1), Specific (0)											
7. Internal (1), External (0)	[speaker]										
8. Internal (1), External (0)	[agent]										
9. Internal (1), External (0)	[target]										
10. Personal (1), Universal (0)	[speaker]										
11. Personal (1), Universal (0)	[agent]										
12. Personal (1), Universal (0)	[target]										
13. Controllable (1), Uncontrollable (0)	[speaker]										
14. Controllable (1), Uncontrollable (0)	[agent]										
15. Controllable (1), Uncontrollable (0)	[target]										

Figure 2.2   Coding templates for use with SPSS or similar software

4. Coding speaker, agent and target

Once all attributions have been extracted, and cause and outcome elements identified, coding can begin. Speaker, agent and target codings can be useful for several reasons. First, the number of times a speaker mentions different agents or targets can show the extent to which the speaker describes himself as an agent (i.e. causing events to occur) rather than a target (being influenced by a particular cause). A simple count can provide an insight into the extent to which the speaker considers or wishes to portray himself as influencing of, rather than being influenced by, specific outcomes. Second, identifying agents the speaker nominates as most likely to influence certain targets is possible. Finally, one can also see the extent to which particular agents and targets are associated with negative or positive outcomes.

Stage one is to code the 'speaker', 'agent' and 'target'. The 'speaker' is the person providing the attribution. The LACS defines an 'agent' as the person, group or entity nominated in the *cause* of the attribution. For example, in the attribution '*I was late because my sister hid my shoes*', the speaker's sister is the agent. The 'target' is the person, group or entity mentioned in the *outcome* of the attribution. For example, in the attribution '*My mum was angry because I was late home*', the speaker's mother is the target. To simplify codings, speaker, agent and target categories are usually restricted to individuals, groups or entities likely to be of interest in that particular investigation. For each category, one can devise one's own codes. For example, when coding attributions from transcripts of family therapy sessions, we used the following codes:

(1) Mother
(2) Father
(3) Eldest child
(4) Second child
(5) Third child
(6) Fourth child
(7) Member of extended family not at the therapy session
(8) Multiple members of the family
(9) Therapist
(0) Someone not a member of the family

So, in the attribution '*My husband finds it very difficult because she (eldest daughter) wants to stay out late at night*', the speaker is the mother (1), the agent would be coded as the eldest daughter (3) and the target is the father (2). However, in the attribution '*I find it difficult to get to sleep because I can't stop thinking about work*', the speaker, who in this case is the father (2) is also the person nominated in the outcome (not being able to sleep) and the cause (thinking about work). Consequently, the speaker, agent and target in this attribution would be coded as the father. The ability to code speaker, agent and target separately is an important component of the LACS and can provide an insight into the causal dynamics between individuals. For instance, in the following attribution, the mother of a 3-year-old girl, sexually abused by her stepfather, is asked about why she thinks the abuse took place, the mother replies: *'She was flirting with him, she knew exactly what she was doing.'* In this attribution the mother perceives her 3-year-old daughter to be the agent (she was flirting) of her own abuse. The stepfather is perceived as the target—his behaviour a consequence of the girl's actions.

Theoretically, any number of speaker, agent and target categories can be coded. In circumstances where attributions are extracted from interview transcripts involving only one speaker, there is evidently no need to code for different speakers. The speaker will always be the same person. In that event, codes are only used to identify agents and targets. The following categories were used with material from selection interviews:

(1) Speaker
(2) Speaker's family
(3) Friends and work colleagues
(4) Education (may include teachers at school or university)
(5) Company or employer
(6) Other

So, for example, in the attribution *'I decided to study law because several of my family are lawyers'*, the target or person involved in the outcome (I decided to study law) would be coded 'Self' (1) and the agent would be coded 'Family' (2). In the attribution: *'My school was very proactive in securing work placements, several of my friends got work that way'*, agent would be 'Education' (4) and target would be 'Friends' (3). The second attribution illustrates one advantage that the LACS has over other similar coding schemes in that it allows the researcher to code attributions where the speaker is neither agent nor target.

5. Coding attributions on causal dimensions

It is worth stressing at this point that attributions are coded from the perspective of the speaker. When coding, use information present in the attribution or surrounding transcript to make a decision. Coding is not done on the basis of what one may think is a true representation of the situation. Coding should represent the meanings a speaker wishes to convey, irrespective of whether or not the coder believes or agrees with what is being said.

The LACS allocates each dimension one of three codes, either a (0), (1) or (2). For example, the stable–unstable dimension would be coded (1) if stable, (0) if unstable, or (2) if one could not decide whether it was stable or unstable. In our experience, up to 20% of attributions are given an undecided code. A researcher might just as easily choose an alternative coding system, for example a 1–7 scale. However, different systems are likely to have different consequences for inter-rater reliability.

Stable (1), unstable (0)

This dimension is applied to the cause element of an attribution. Causes can be coded as either stable (1) or unstable (0). If one really cannot decide whether a speaker believes a cause to be stable or unstable, use the code (2).

Stable causes are those that are likely to continue to influence outcomes in the future. Stable causes do not change in the short term. Unstable causes are typically transitory factors that will not influence outcomes very far into the future. For example, take the following attribution taken from a job interview: *'I'm not particularly good in large groups of people, so I'm looking for a job which will allow me to work by myself.'* We would code the cause in this attribution as stable (1); the speaker identifies the cause to be personal characteristic, which do not usually change in the short term.

A stable cause can also be a one-off event which continues to influence the speaker. Think about the example, *'Deciding to go to America that summer really opened opportunities for me. I now know I want to become a geologist.'* Although the cause (deciding to go to America) is an isolated event, it continues to influence the speaker's choice of career.

In the next example, the cause appears to have relatively short-term effects on subsequent outcomes, so we would code it unstable (0). *'I decided not to apply to that company, because I wanted to go travelling that summer'* would be coded unstable, because one has no evidence to suggest that the cause continues to have an effect. Similarly, *'I didn't do too well that year, because I had glandular fever'* would be coded unstable because the speaker describes the outcome in terms of a particular year. Realistically, having glandular fever could have had a more long-term influence on this individual's choice of university and subsequent job opportunities, but the task of the coder is to use *information that is present in the attribution*. In this attribution the speaker provides no additional information that having glandular fever has had long-term repercussions, therefore it is coded unstable.

The following are provided as practise examples. Try coding them for 'stable' and 'unstable' then compare your codings with the ones that the authors have agreed at the end of the chapter (see 'Practise examples' on p. 68):

(1) *'My teachers couldn't believe it, it was so unlike me to fail an exam like that.'*
(2) *'I used to go out all the time. I think it was just a phase of growing up.'*
(3) *'I wasn't all that surprised at the result, I've never been all that good at chemistry'.*
(4) *'My teacher left halfway through the year which made things difficult.'*
(5) *'She helped me get the job because she thought I had potential.'*
(6) *'Jane has really changed since she went to assertiveness classes.'*

Global (1), specific (0)

The global–specific dimension is applied to the cause element of an attribution. Causes can be coded as either global (1) or specific (0). If deciding whether a speaker believes a cause to be global or specific is impossible, use the code (2).

Global causes are those that are likely to have a significant impact on several different outcomes. Specific causes, on the other hand, are more often found in descriptions of one-off events. Specific causes are unlikely to have repercussions beyond the one identified in the attribution being coded.

The following example comes from another job interview: '*I think managing to get into Cambridge, has opened doors for me.*' We would code the cause in this attribution as global (1); it is likely that the speaker believes that having been to Cambridge will continue to help him or her do well in the jobs market. In this attribution from a clinical interview, the speaker is making an attribution about his or her father's second marriage: '*Dad wanted to have a normal life and be happy, so he got married*'. We would code the cause in this attribution as global (1); the desire for happiness and a normal life is likely to be a major influence on several important aspects of this man's life. In contrast, we would code the cause of the next attribution as specific (0): '*I go to quite a number of plays and films, because I belong to the university Arts Society*'. We have no reason to believe that the speaker thinks membership of the Arts Society influences anything other than the number of films and plays he or she goes to. Here is another attribution with a specific (0) cause: '*I woke up feeling sick yesterday, so I didn't go into work.*' In this case the speaker is describing a one-off incident. The fact that the speaker felt ill has led that person to miss a day's work. We code the cause as specific (0) because nothing in the attribution suggests any other significant consequences of feeling sick. In our experience, the global–specific dimension is the one that people have the most problems coding. When we have compared codings of the same attributions done by different people, the global–specific dimension produces the highest number of disagreements. One way of keeping disagreements to a minimum may be to decide, before starting to code, which are the important outcomes in your particular study. For example, if one were interested in health behaviours, one might decide that *any* causes a speaker provides for outcomes concerned with health behaviour would be coded as global (1). Applying a definition consistently to your material is often more important than using the same definition in a very different study.

The following examples come from selection interviews. In this research the definition of a global cause was adapted slightly. It was decided to code global any cause that could be considered to have an important influence on an individual's career, whether it concerned choices available, likely level of future seniority, employability, or the person's marketability.

(1) *'Hitchhiking through Australia made me really question whether I wanted to work for a large organisation.'*
(2) *'I got the lead in the play because of all the hard work I put in.'*
(3) *'They elected me captain because they thought I could do the job.'*
(4) *'Being a school representative meant that I had to meet quite a few different people.'*
(5) *'Unfortunately my first year grades weren't too good, I suppose I'd spent too much time getting involved in sports.'*
(6) *'I spent the summer working for another law firm, it gave me an invaluable insight into how the profession works.'*

Internal (1), external (0)

This dimension is applied to the cause element of an attribution. Causes can be coded as either internal (1) or external (0). If saying whether a cause is internal or external is impossible, use the code (2).

As the framework above shows, one can use the internal–external dimension to code the same cause from three different perspectives. Attributions in which a speaker identifies an agent (someone identified in the cause of the attribution) and a target (someone mentioned in the outcome of the attribution) can be given three different internal–external codings. For example, if a mother makes the attribution *'She (daughter) doesn't like school, because the other children bully her'*, her daughter would be identified as target and the other children as agent. The cause could then be coded separately for Mother (speaker), Daughter (target) and Children (agent).

Internal causes are those believed to originate from within the person being coded. External causes usually describe characteristics of other people, or a set of circumstances. This internal–external distinction is the same as the one used by Martin Seligman in his learned helplessness model of depression. Internal causes describe factors that reside 'within the skin', external causes describe factors 'outside the skin'.

This example comes from a job interview: *'The company took me on, because I knew about that particular computer system.'* The cause in this attribution would be coded internal (1) because the cause is the speaker's knowledge. Similarly, the cause in the attribution 'I failed the exam because I didn't do enough preparation' would be coded internal because the cause is the speaker's failure to act.

In the examples 'None of the class did very well on that particular exam, because the teacher gave us the wrong material to learn' and 'I learnt a lot from working alongside specialists in the area', both causes would be coded external (0). Each cause is firmly located outside of the speaker.

PRACTISE EXAMPLES

(1)   'My father suggested that I try for law.'

(2)   'The course appealed to me because it had a large practical component.'

(3)   'They decided to give me the job because I'd had so much experience.'

(4)   (How come you were asked to go to France?) 'I just happened to be in the right place at the right time.'

(5)   'I managed to persuade the team to change strategy, but it required a special effort.'

(6)   'It was a wonderful opportunity because it meant that we could all travel to America.'

Personal (1), universal (0)

To code this dimension, one needs to look at all three elements of an attribution: the cause, the link and the outcome. Attributions can be coded as either personal (1) or universal (0). If saying whether an attribution is personal or universal is impossible, use the code (2).

As with the internal–external dimension, one can code the same attribution on the personal–universal dimension from three different perspectives. Attributions in which a speaker identifies an agent (someone identified in the cause of the attribution) and a target (someone mentioned in the outcome of the attribution) can be given three different personal–universal codings. The personal–universal dimension was originally created to pick out attributions in which people identified something different, special or unique about someone else in the family. We have also found the dimension to be useful in a work context. The personal/universal coding can distinguish between attributions in which some people want to set themselves apart from a work group, and attributions where they describe their actions as normal.

An attribution is coded personal (1) when either the cause, the outcome, or the link between the cause and outcome contains information concerning something unique or idiosyncratic about the person being coded. This next example comes from a graduate recruitment interview: *'They chose me, because I had captained the school hockey team.'* This attribution would be coded personal (1) because the interviewee is describing something about herself that she considers to be distinct, not typical of other graduates applying for a job. Similarly, the attribution *'Backpacking through Africa gave me a rare insight into other cultures'* would be coded personal (1) because the speaker believes that those experiences set him or her apart from most other people in the same position.

An attribution is coded universal (0) when nothing in the cause, the outcome or the link between the two suggests anything distinctive about that person. In attributions coded universal (0), the speaker gives no reason to believe that his or her behaviour is any different from any other person in the reference group. This example comes from another graduate recruitment interview: *'I wanted to do criminal law, I guess at that age you're rather naive and utopian.'* This attribution would be coded universal (0) because we can reasonably assume that the candidate thinks his or her behaviour is typical of anybody of that age.

Remember that attributions are coded from the speaker's perspective. Therefore, although in the coder's opinion the action describes something highly idiosyncratic about the person, if the speaker believes his or her behaviour to be normal, the attribution would be coded universal (0). Look at the following example (somewhat unlikely in a selection interview): *'It was nothing special, my friends were taking soft drugs so I decided to get involved.'* As a coder who thinks that the desire to take illegal psychoactive drugs suggests something unusual about a person, one may want to code this attribution as personal (1). However, because the speaker clearly thinks that his or her behaviour was nothing out of the ordinary, the attribution should be coded universal (0).

PRACTISE EXAMPLES

(1) *'I reckon that I'm suited to a job which involves travel because I've done so much travelling in the past.'*

(2) *'He was nervous about getting into the water, so I did what anybody would do, I talked him through and helped him to relax.'*

(3) *(Why were you chosen?) 'I guess that my interest in Science Fiction made me a little different from the rest of the group.'*

(4) *'I decided to study Physics because my "A" Level teacher really interested us in the subject.'*

(5) *'I realised too late that I didn't really know enough about the subject, so I had to carry on.'*

(6) *'My friends think I'm a little strange because I enjoy studying.'*

Controllable (1), uncontrollable (0)

To code this dimension, one needs to look at all three elements of an attribution (cause, link and outcome) again. Attributions can be coded as either controllable (1) or uncontrollable (0). If saying whether an attribution is controllable or uncontrollable is impossible, use the code (2).

As with the previous two dimensions, one can code the same attribution on the controllable–uncontrollable dimension from three different perspectives. Attributions in which a speaker identifies an agent (someone identified in the cause of the attribution) and a target (someone mentioned in the outcome of the attribution) can be given three different controllable/uncontrollable codings.

An attribution is coded controllable (1) if the speaker thinks he or she could have influenced the outcome without having to exert some exceptional effort. Clues about whether the outcome could have been influenced can be found in any part of the attribution sequence of cause, link and outcome.

If the speaker believes that the cause, link, outcome sequence was an inevitable sequence of events that could not have been influenced in any circumstances, then the attribution is coded uncontrollable (0). This example of an attribution comes from a selection interview: *'I failed Chemistry, because I spent too much time on my duties as Secretary for the Athletics Society.'* One would code this as controllable because the speaker clearly believes that she could have chosen to spend her time doing other things, and therefore have influenced the outcome of the attribution. Similarly the attribution *'I went on writing letters and in the end they decided to offer me the place'* would be coded controllable. The next example attribution is less straightforward, but clearly should be coded controllable: *'They were renovating the school library, so I asked if I could use the one at the local college'.* The speaker evidently has no control over decisions to renovate the library. However, given the problem, he decided to pursue alternative arrangements. The speaker did have control over whether he made a request to his local college library.

We would code an attribution as uncontrollable (0) if we have good reason to believe that the speaker perceives the outcome to be inevitable or not open to influence. For example, the attribution *'I missed the deadline for the application because I came down with 'flu'* would be coded uncontrollable. In general, people do not believe they can control whether or not they fall victim to a virus. The same applies to the next example: *'None of my class did well in that subject because the teacher followed the wrong syllabus.'* We would code this uncontrollable (0) because the speaker clearly believes that failure was entirely due to the teacher. However, if we were coding the controllable–uncontrollable from the perspective of the agent (someone identified in the cause of the attribution), we would code it controllable (1). The speaker appears to think that the teacher could have taught the right syllabus if he or she had chosen to.

PRACTISE EXAMPLES

(1) *'I decided to join the orchestra because it meant that I could practise with other people.'*

(2) *'My friend persuaded me to apply for the position.'*

(3) *'Everyone was so enthusiastic I felt that I was being pushed into the decision.'*

(4)   '*I got all the books I could on the subject so that I would be really prepared.*'

(5)   '*In the end the elections didn't go so well, because the printers were too late delivering the leaflets.*'

(6)   '*I've always enjoyed history because my aunt works in the local museum.*'

Other dimensions

Besides the coding dimensions specified here, researchers can include other dimensions of theoretical relevance to their data. For example, one may want to think about coding attributions for valency, i.e. whether the outcome or event being described in the attribution is a positive or negative one. Some researchers have suggested that people make different types of attributions for positive and negative outcomes, and that these should be coded and analysed separately. Outcomes can be coded as either positive (2), neutral (1) or negative (0).

In an investigation of work-related attributions made by people from different cultures, we coded the topic of each attribution produced by German and British engineers. A full account of the research appears in Chapter 4. We wanted to identify the areas of organisational functioning that engineers discussed during semi-structured interviews, and how they described them in terms of causal relationships. However, developing and reporting new dimensions has inevitable drawbacks when it comes to the generalisability of your data. Attribution theory is most often used as a theoretical tool in the context of established dimensions, including those used in the LACS. Although potentially enriching the field, incorporating unfamiliar and less traditional coding categories needs to be done within the context of some theoretical justification.

PRACTISE EXAMPLES

The first example is taken from a selection interview:

INTERVIEWER: *OK. What would you say makes you different from perhaps other people?*

CANDIDATE: *Right well I think I'm, I think I'm quite a curious person and I also think I'm quite an ambitious person so I'd say on my cycling trips it was the general spirit of adventure, a spirit of, which appealed to me, a spirit of jumping a little into the unknown, you know, you're not quite sure of what's waiting ahead of you so whereas I think a lot of people are much more reluctant and don't like, don't like to have to deal with, with things that are new or things that are unexpected I think I do.*

INTERVIEWER: *OK.*

CANDIDATE: *So this is why I'd say I'd go on a, on a cycling trip round, round Spain or wherever rather than just go there on a, you know, on a package trip. That's why I'd rather go there by bike and go by car and whatever really. So I'd say it's a spirit of, of excitement and of wanting to find something new. And also a spirit of achievement as well I would say, it is quite satisfying to feel you've cycled round most of Europe really.*

INTERVIEWER: *OK but obviously during this time you must have come across a few, a few difficulties and problems . . .*

CANDIDATE: *Yes sure well on my cycling trips we had a few technical problems, bikes broke down more frequently than we had anticipated but on, on shall we say a non-technical point of view I'd say that a trip like that does require a certain degree of commitment because it can be easy to lose motivation. I mean in Belgium for example it's very windy and it can get quite cold and wet even in the summer and, you know, you're cycling down a road where, where trees don't even grow straight because it's, it's so windy at times that some- times you think I could be on holiday in Tenerife with my friends, but you're doing something different.*

INTERVIEWER: *What do you, how do you actually overcome that?*

CANDIDATE: *Well you are, deep inside you are aware of the fact that it's the sort of experience that actually gives you a kick and you're aware of the fact that, you know, lack of motivation or whatever is, is just temporary and you'll soon glean the satisfaction from doing what it is you are doing and you're aware of that.*

INTERVIEWER: *OK. Have you had problems, you know, with the motivation of other people with perhaps this person or anyone else you've been cycling with?*

CANDIDATE: *Well when you go on a trip like that you know you're only going with one other person so you make sure that the person you go with is as keen to do it as you are. Having said that on one occasion we went on a trip where we wanted to cycle down to the south of Italy and come back up to Yugoslavia. And four days into our trip he decided that he was ill which he probably was to a certain extent so he got onto a train down to southern Yugoslavia where his parents were staying on holiday. He said to me 'Why don't you cycle down?' and this would have been, I don't know, six or seven hundred miles away 'Why don't you cycle down and then we'll cycle back up together?' I agreed to do that and I cycled down and of course he couldn't be bothered to cycle back so it was obviously a bit of a, a bit of a disappointment.*

INTERVIEWER: *So what did you do then?*

CANDIDATE: *Well I tried to talk him into it but I was aware of the fact that if he didn't want to do it there wouldn't be that much point in me trying to push him too hard 'cos he'd probably set off and after a couple of days he'd, he'd just give up so I think when it comes to motivating other people you have to also look at what, what the circumstances are and in that particular case I felt that, you know, it probably wasn't worth pursuing the matter too much, you know, either he wanted to do it, if he didn't want to do it then I have to accept that ultimately and, you know, just obviously I was disappointed but I didn't feel there was that much I could do about it other than try to remind him of why it is we wanted to do that in the first place and why it is he should maybe see that, that these things are worth doing.*

The following attributions have been identified in the text:

INTERVIEWER: / *OK. What would you say makes you different from perhaps other people?*

CANDIDATE: *Right well I think I'm, (1)* ← *I think I'm quite a curious person and (2)* ← *I also think I'm quite an ambitious person so I'd say on my cycling trips it was general spirit of adventure, a spirit of, which appealed to me, a spirit of jumping a little into the unknown, you know, you're not quite sure of what's waiting ahead of you so whereas (3)* ← *[I think a lot of people are much more reluctant and don't like, don't like to have to deal with, with things that are new or things that are unexpected I think I do.] (4)* →

INTERVIEWER: *OK.*

CANDIDATE: *So this is why I'd say I'd go on a, on a cycling trip round, round Spain or wherever rather than just go there on a, you know,* on a package trip. / (5) / That's why I'd rather go there by bike and go by car and whatever really.← So I'd say it's a spirit of, of excitement and of wanting to find something new. (6) ← And also a spirit of achievement as well (7) I would say, it is quite satisfying ← to feel you've cycled round most of Europe really

INTERVIEWER: OK but obviously during this time you must have come across a few, a few difficulties and problems . . .

CANDIDATE: Yes sure well on my cycling trips we had a few technical problems, bikes broke down more frequently than we had anticipated but on, on shall we say a non-technical point of view (8) / I'd say that a trip like that does require a certain degree of commitment ← because it can be easy to lose motivation. (9) I mean in Belgium for example it's very windy and it can get quite cold and wet even in the summer and, you know, you're cycling down a road where, where trees don't even grow straight (because it's, it's so windy at times) → that sometimes you think I could be on holiday in Tenerife with my friends / but you're doing something different.

INTERVIEWER: What do you, (10) / how do you actually overcome that?

CANDIDATE: ← Well you are, deep inside you are aware of the fact that it's the sort of experience that actually gives you a kick and (11) ← you're aware of the fact that, you know, lack of motivation or whatever is, is just temporary and you'll soon glean the satisfaction from doing what it is you are doing and you're aware of that.

INTERVIEWER: OK. Have you had problems, you know, with the motivation of other people with perhaps this person or anyone else you've been cycling with?

CANDIDATE: (12) Well when you go on a trip like that you know you're only going with one other person → so you make sure that the person you go with is actually as keen to do it as you are. / So on this particular occasion the partner I chose wouldn't have had any major lacks of motivation although having said that on one occasion we went on a trip and we wanted to cycle down to the south of Italy and come up, come back up to Yugoslavia and four days into like, into our trip he decided that he was, he was ill which he probably was to a certain extent and he got onto a train down to southern Yugoslavia where his parents were staying on holiday and he said to me 'Why don't you cycle down?' and this would have been, I don't know, six or seven hundred miles away 'Why don't you cycle down *and then we'll cycle back up together?' and I agreed to do that and I cycle down and of course (13) he couldn't be bothered to cycle back* → *so it was obviously a bit of a, a bit of a disappointment.*

INTERVIEWER: *So what did you do then?*

CANDIDATE: *Well I tried to talk him into it but I was aware of the fact that (14) if he didn't want to do it* → *there wouldn't be that much point in me trying to push him too hard* ← *(15) 'cos he'd probably set off and after a couple of days he'd, he'd just give up so I think when it comes to motivating other people you have to also look at what, what the circumstances are and in that particular case I felt that, you know, it probably wasn't worth pursuing the matter too much, you know, either he wanted to do it, (16) if he didn't want to do it* → *then I have to accept that ultimately and, you know, just obviously I was disappointed but I didn't feel there was that much I could do about it other than try to remind him of why it is we wanted to do that in the first place and why it is he should maybe see that, that these things are worth doing.*

The following example comes from an interview with a mother about her 3-year-old son. It was part of a study investigating the attributions that parents made for the good and bad behaviour of their young children. It is a good example because it illustrates how as a coder we may not necessarily agree with the sentiments of the speaker, but we must try to code the attributions from the speaker's perspective.

And me and my friend ran out. We were just stood there, we couldn't say nowt, there's Sam just throwing bricks through her windows. He was threeish . . . I said 'what are you doing?'. He said he wanted to know what it sounded like. I mean, we couldn't play hell with him because we were both stood there gobsmacked. And I just turned away 'cos I started laughing. (How many windows went?) *Four or five. Mary couldn't do nowt. Anyway, in the end I went a bit mad. I couldn't go too mad 'cos I thought it was funny myself. There was only him there, it was only the garden next door, and they were only little stones, little brick stones.*

The following attributional statements can be extracted:

And me and my friend ran out. We were just stood there, we couldn't say nowt, there's Sam just throwing bricks through her windows. He was threeish . . . I said 'what are you doing?'. He said he wanted to know what it sounded like. (1) / I mean, we couldn't play hell with him ← because we were both stood there gobsmacked. And (2) I just turned away ← 'cos I started laughing. (How many windows went?) Four or five. Mary couldn't do nowt. Anyway, in the end I went a bit mad. (3) I couldn't go too mad ← 'cos I thought it was funny myself. (4) ← There was only him there /, (5) it was only the garden next door /, and (6) they were only little stones, little brick stones. /

The list of attributions to be coded is:

(1) *I mean, we couldn't play hell with him because we were both stood there gobsmacked*
(2) *I just turned away 'cos I started laughing*
(3) *I couldn't go too mad 'cos I thought it was funny myself*
(4) *(I thought it was funny myself) There was only him there*
(5) *(I thought it was funny myself) it was only the garden next door*
(6) *(I thought it was funny myself) they were only little stones, little brick stones*

For the purposes of coding speaker, agent and target, mother has been given the code (1), and her child (3). Figure 2.3 shows the codings.

6. Analysis

The LACS involves coding qualitative material. Coders need to make subjective judgements about each dimension. The definition of each dimension on the LACS has been worded to reduce to a minimum the extent to which coders have to rely on their own judgement to arrive at a decision. The extent to which we have been successful can be measured by looking at what is usually called inter-rater reliability. Quite simply, inter-rater reliability looks at the amount of agreement between two or more people who have coded the same material. We are concerned with the extent to which these attributions convey the same meaning to different listeners.

It is generally good practice to check that attributions have not been coded in some completely idiosyncratic manner. Justifying a comparison of your material with other attribution studies

1. Attribution number			1	2	3	4	5	6	7	8	9	10
2. Speaker			1	1	1	1	1	1				
3. Agent			1	1	1	3	3	3				
4. Target			1	1	1	1	1	1				
5. Stable (1), Unstable (0)			0	0	0	0	0	0				
6. Global (1), Specific (0)			0	0	0	0	0	0				
7. Internal (1), External (0)	[speaker]		0	1	1	0	0	0				
8. Internal (1), External (0)	[agent]		0	1	1	1	0	0				
9. Internal (1), External (0)	[target]		0	1	1	0	0	0				
10. Personal (1), Universal (0)	[speaker]		0	0	0	0	0	0				
11. Personal (1), Universal (0)	[agent]		0	0	0	0	0	0				
12. Personal (1), Universal (0)	[target]		0	0	0	0	0	0				
13. Controllable (1), Uncontrollable (0)	[speaker]		0	0	0	0	0	0				
14. Controllable (1), Uncontrollable (0)	[agent]		0	0	0	0	0	0				
15. Controllable (1), Uncontrollable (0)	[target]		0	0	0	0	0	0				

Figure 2.3   Codings of the six attributions

would be difficult if it could not be shown that your use of the definitions is comparable. Of course the use of independent coders increases the cost of the research. Not only must the researcher find people willing to act as coders and provide incentives, possibly payment, if necessary, but coders must also be trained in the use of the LACS to ensure adequate levels of reliability. This will inevitably increase the time a researcher will need to complete a project. To make the process less complex, having a random sample of your attributions coded by a second person, rather than having the whole lot done twice, can be effective.

A statistic called Cohen's kappa can be used to assess reliability for approximately 20–30% of the attributions extracted for a study. Usually, values of kappa above 0.4 are considered acceptable, whereas those above 0.7 are good. Typically, all causal dimensions as defined in the LACS have demonstrated acceptable or good levels of reliability. However, the stable–global and personal–universal dimensions usually prove least reliable. Moreover, coding the controllable–uncontrollable dimension can be difficult when the agent or target is inanimate, for example in the case of 'organisation' or 'education'.

The data set from even a relatively small-scale analysis of attributions can prove large. We have found it useful to enter coded data into a computer software package such as the Statistical Package for the Social Sciences (SPSS). These packages make it possible to identify different subsets of attributions for analysis. For example, there may be some sound theoretical reason for examining attributions in which the speaker is agent and outcomes are positive. More simply, statistical packages allow the calculation of percentages of attributions given different codes on each dimension. For example, one may wish to know what percentage of all attributions made by a particular speaker were coded as stable rather than unstable.

What follows is another worked example, this time taken from a clinical interview in a family therapy setting.

MOTHER: *On Thursday morning she howled the place down for this hairbrush and I searched everywhere. I went into Sarah's room, Jamie's room, Helen's room. I looked everywhere. I was running round like a ding-bat while she roared the place down, really screaming. You (father) came down and you said if this nonsense doesn't stop immediately I'm going to thrash you. You (father) went back upstairs, you went into the bathroom and started washing and it continued. It went on for about three quarters of an hour. . .*

FATHER: *And Jamie had an exam that day, you know, and she (Helen) knew this. This is the point. If she knows anything is going to happen she will deliberately disrupt the household. I mean you can see it happening . . . she plans it and she enjoys it, there's no question about it.*

THERAPIST: *What happened to your brush that day?*

HELEN: *I'm not saying anything.*

THERAPIST: *Well who did take it in fact?*

FATHER: *She (Helen) had, she hides it.*

MOTHER: *Well I can tell you, in the end Helen did get a smack and she got a black eye.*

HELEN: *No I didn't get a smack, I got a kick in the face mum.*
FATHER: *No you didn't that's not true.*
HELEN: *Yes it is.*
FATHER: *I'm sorry, but I'm not going to sit and listen to that nonsense . . .*
THERAPIST: *From whom did she get the kick?*
FATHER: *Well me. But she'll do it again tomorrow.*
THERAPIST: *How did it happen—so we can put the record straight?*
FATHER: *Well she was on the floor, and this had been going on for half an hour. I mean I don't keep records of these things, but you have to understand that this is not just one morning, this is a whole series of mornings until it gets to the point where it's near to murder and that's probably where we are now. And if she had carried on with it I probably would have murdered her. You have to understand that I'm not kidding with these things.*
THERAPIST: *What happened then?*
MOTHER: *You attacked Jamie, you said where is her hairbrush? And he said I haven't got it . . .*
Father: *I pulled Jamie off because he's a big boy, he's taller than me, but he's the best one to handle. And she doesn't deserve it the way he treats her, he's the most attentive and they argue in the normal family way. But he cares for her and will do things for her, but she just consistently keeps provoking him to the point where we are both going to murder her one day.*
THERAPIST: *That must have been quite frightening for things to have got to such a pitch.*
MOTHER: *It was . . .*
FATHER: *For me too . . . . I have to lead a normal life, I mean I try to . . .*
Mother: *I was trying to . . . I try to say to Peter (father) you know, keep calm because Peter never comes downstairs in the morning. He came down twice and on the third occasion he came down and he bashed them and he also bashed Jamie because he said well Jamie or Sarah must have this hairbrush that's causing such a scene. And you gave Jamie such a wallop across the shoulder to get at her . . .*
FATHER: *And just to describe the actual incident where Helen has told you that I kicked her in the face, that's an absolute and total lie. She was lying on the floor and I did this with my foot. And now I mean if I want to kick her and hurt her I can, I played sports . . .*

HELEN: *Well you got me with your shoe.*

FATHER: *I've played sports and if I want to hurt someone I can. And what I did, she was resting on the floor, lying on the floor just in a very provocative pose and her arm was there and I hit her with my foot and her own hand went into her eye. Now they are the facts and I don't care what anybody says. And I mean this is the typically provocative way in which she distorts the truth. I kicked her in the face . . . it's infuriating!*

The following attributions were identified in the text:

MOTHER: *(1) On Thursday morning she howled the place down for this hairbrush → and I searched everywhere /. I went into Sarah's room, Jamie's room, Helen's room. I looked everywhere. (2) / I was running round like a ding-bat ← while she roared the place down, really screaming. You (father) came down and you said if this nonsense doesn't stop immediately I'm going to thrash you. You (father) went back upstairs, you went into the bathroom and started washing and it continued. It went on for about three quarters of an hour . . .*

FATHER: *And Jamie had an exam that day, you know, and she (Helen) knew this. This is the point. (3) If she knows anything is going to happen → she will deliberately disrupt the household. / I mean you can see it happening . . . she plans it and she enjoys it, there's no question about it.*

THERAPIST: *What happened to your brush that day?*

HELEN: *I'm not saying anything.*

THERAPIST: *Well who did take it in fact?*

FATHER: *She (Helen) had, she hides it.*

MOTHER: *Well I can tell you, in the end Helen did get a smack and she got a black eye.*

HELEN: *No I didn't get a smack, I got a kick in the face mum.*

FATHER: *No you didn't that's not true.*

HELEN: *Yes it is.*

FATHER: *I'm sorry, but I'm not going to sit and listen to that nonsense . . .*

THERAPIST: *From whom did she get the kick?*

FATHER: *Well me. But she'll do it again tomorrow.*

THERAPIST: *How did it happen – so we can put the record straight?*

FATHER: *Well she was on the floor, and this had been going on for half an hour. I mean I don't keep records of these things, but you have to understand that (4)* this is not just one morning, this is a whole series of mornings *→ until it gets to the point where it's near to murder and that's probably where we are now /. And if she had carried on with it I probably would have murdered her. You have to understand that I'm not kidding with these things.*

THERAPIST: *What happened then?*

MOTHER: *You attacked Jamie, you said where is her hairbrush? And he said I haven't got it . . .*

FATHER: *(5) / I pulled Jamie off ←* because he's a big boy, he's taller than me, but he's the best one to handle. *And she doesn't deserve it the way he treats her, he's the most attentive and they argue in the normal family way. (6)* But he cares for her *→ and will do things for her /, but (7)* she just consistently keeps provoking him *→ to the point where we are both going to murder her one day /.*

THERAPIST: *That must have been quite frightening for things to have got to such a pitch.*

MOTHER: *It was . . .*

FATHER: *For me too . . . I have to lead a normal life, I mean I try to . . .*

MOTHER: *(8) / I was trying to . . . I try to say to Peter (father) you know, keep calm ←* because Peter never comes downstairs in the morning. *He came down twice and on the third occasion he came down and he bashed them and (9)* / he also bashed Jamie ←* because he said well Jamie or Sarah must have this hairbrush that's causing such a scene. *And you gave Jamie such a wallop across the shoulder to get at her . . .*

FATHER: *And just to describe the actual incident where Helen has told you that I kicked her in the face, that's an absolute and total lie. She was lying on the floor and I did this with my foot. And now I mean if I want to kick her and hurt her I can, I played sports . . .*

HELEN: *Well you got me with your shoe.*

---

* Note that this is a reported attribution, that is a statement of cause and effect that was originally produced by the father and is now reported by the mother. Usually we do not extract or code such attributions. Relatively few have been produced in the research material we have explored so far. This is not to say that other researchers may not find an investigation of attributions produced by one individual or group interesting or potentially worth while.

FATHER: (10) *I've played sports* → *and if I want to hurt someone I can* /. *And what I did, (11) she was resting on the floor, lying on the floor just in a very provocative pose and her arm was there* → *and (12) I hit her with my foot* → *and her own hand went into her eye* /. *Now they are the facts and I don't care what anybody says. And I mean (13) this is the typically provocative way in which she distorts the truth.* → *I kicked her in the face . . . it's infuriating!* /

EXTRACTED ATTRIBUTIONS

(1)   *On Thursday morning she howled the place down for this hairbrush* → *and I searched everywhere* /.

(2)   / *I was running round like a ding-bat* ← *while she roared the place down, really screaming.*

(3)   *If she knows anything is going to happen* → *she will deliberately disrupt the household.* /

(4)   *this is not just one morning, this is a whole series of mornings* → *until it gets to the point where it's near to murder and that's probably where we are now* /.

(5)   / *I pulled Jamie off* ← *because he's a big boy, he's taller than me, but he's the best one to handle.*

(6)   *But he cares for her* → *and will do things for her* /.

(7)   *she just consistently keeps provoking him* → *to the point where we are both going to murder her one day* /.

(8)   / *I was trying to . . . I try to say to Peter (father) you know, keep calm* ← *because Peter never comes downstairs in the morning.*

(9)   / *he also bashed Jamie* ← *because he said well Jamie or Sarah must have this hairbrush that's causing such a scene.*

(10) *I've played sports* → *and if I want to hurt someone I can* /.

(11)* *she was resting on the floor, lying on the floor just in a very provocative pose and her arm was there (and I hit her with my foot)* → *and her own hand went into her eye* /.

(12)* *I hit her with my foot* → *and her own hand went into her eye* /.

---

* This is quite a complex attribution. A decision was taken to extract two separate causes for the same outcome (the black eye), because it seems clear from the passage, that although the father acknowledges that his foot has hit his daughter's face, he is also attributing blame to her for lying on the floor in a 'provocative' manner.

	1	2	3	4	5	6	7	8	9	10
1. Attribution number	1	2	3	4	5	6	7	8	9	10
2. Speaker	1	1	2	2	2	2	2	1	1	2
3. Agent	5	5	5	5	2	3	5	2	2	2
4. Target	1	1	5	2	3	5	3	1	3	2
5. Stable (1), Unstable (0)	0	0	1	1	0	1	1	1	0	1
6. Global (1), Specific (0)	0	0	1	1	0	1	1	0	0	0
7. Internal (1), External (0) [speaker]	0	0	0	0	0	0	0	0	0	1
8. Internal (1), External (0) [agent]	1	1	1	1	0	1	1	1	1	1
9. Internal (1), External (0) [target]	0	0	1	0	1	0	0	0	1	1
10. Personal (1), Universal (0) [speaker]	0	0	0	1	0	0	0	0	0	1
11. Personal (1), Universal (0) [agent]	1	1	1	1	0	1	1	1	0	1
12. Personal (1), Universal (0) [target]	0	0	1	1	1	0	0	0	0	1
13. Controllable (1), Uncontrollable (0) [speaker]	0	0	0	0	1	0	0	1	0	1
14. Controllable (1), Uncontrollable (0) [agent]	1	1	1	1	1	1	1	2	1	1
15. Controllable (1), Uncontrollable (0) [target]	0	0	1	0	0	0	0	1	0	1

Figure 2.4 (above and opposite) Codings of the 13 attributions

(13)   <u>this is the typically provocative way in which she distorts the truth.</u> → I kicked her in the face . . . it's infuriating! /

For the purposes of coding speaker, agent and target, as before we have used (1) for mother, (2) for father, (3) for eldest child, (4) for second child, etc. Figure 2.4 shows the coding.

ADVANTAGES AND DISADVANTAGES OF THE LACS METHOD

It is not always justifiable to assume that spoken attributions accurately reflect internal thought processes. When using the LACS, it is important to remember that attributional coding reflects the complex, dynamic way in which people manipulate public attributions to convey particular impressions.

		11	12	13	14	15	16	17	18	19	20
1. Attribution number		11	12	13							
2. Speaker		2	2	2							
3. Agent		5	2	5							
4. Target		2	5	2							
5. Stable (1), Unstable (0)		0	0	1							
6. Global (1), Specific (0)		0	0	1							
7. Internal (1), External (0)	[speaker]	0	1	0							
8. Internal (1), External (0)	[agent]	1	1	1							
9. Internal (1), External (0)	[target]	0	0	0							
10. Personal (1), Universal (0)	[speaker]	0	0	0							
11. Personal (1), Universal (0)	[agent]	1	0	1							
12. Personal (1), Universal (0)	[target]	0	0	0							
13. Controllable (1), Uncontrollable (0)	[speaker]	0	0	0							
14. Controllable (1), Uncontrollable (0)	[agent]	1	0	1							
15. Controllable (1), Uncontrollable (0)	[target]	0	0	0							

Researchers need to weigh the advantages and disadvantages of any method before they decide which one best suits their particular research question or theoretical perspective. The disadvantages of attributional coding lie with its complexity and the fact that it is time-consuming and therefore costly to undertake. It will also take time and possibly training before the newcomer feels entirely confident with the method and able to achieve adequate levels of reliability. Consequently, attributional coding should not be viewed as a method that can be learned and then applied over a very short time. Similarly, attributional coding, like many other qualitative methods, depends upon transcribed material and, as a result, can prove costly. On a positive note, the growing body of transcribed material now being made available through groups such as the Economic and Social Research Council should provide one means of reducing costs, as could greater sharing of material by qualitative researchers.

These problems aside, we have found attributional coding to be very rewarding, and a valuable means of exploring how individuals make sense of their world. The LACS system can be used by researchers working in either qualitative or quantitative disciplines. The fact that *both* qualitative and quantitative researchers can use the method is in itself a positive advantage.

In conclusion, attributional coding enables researchers to use naturalistic data, i.e. the attributions that individuals produce themselves for real events rather than hypothetical scenarios created by researchers. The sensitivity of the method means that the dynamic interplay between two people negotiating the most likely causes of events can be explored. Although attributional coding requires practice, perseverance can be rewarded with a more detailed insight into relationships between attributions, cognitions and behaviour.

APPENDIX: EXTRACTED ATTRIBUTIONS

(1) If you smack Karen, → that just makes the problem worse /. (2) When she's naughty → she'll defy you all the way and she won't give in /. And (3) if you smack her → [(4) because you've had enough of her defying you and telling you like] → she'll say 'I don't love you, I'm going to run away' /. (5) Well all kids say things like that → so you take them in your stride /. But (6) if she carries on to the extent that → [(7) you have to give her a smack] / (8) ← ['cos she's really getting defiant here,] she'll sit and scream and carry on and things like that / (9) / She'll throw herself into a tantrum so much → that you feel like strangling her /. But you don't strangle her, (10) / you have to give her a cuddle ← because she can't understand that when she's naughty and you're upset you can't cuddle her.

(11) / 'Cos I put her into bed once ← with her being misbehaved and (12) / I couldn't do it no more ← 'cos she wrecked the bedroom. She threw everything on the floor, she tore all the wall paper off the wall, kicked the door and screamed. (13) And all I could do was hear her screaming and carrying on. → And [(14) it made me feel like going up and really smacking her hard →] /. So now I can't do that /.

Notice that, in this excerpt from a mother of a 5-year-old girl, extracting attributions is not a clear-cut exercise. In several examples, what is clearly the outcome of one cause also acts as the cause of a second outcome. We can describe these as causal sequences. The best way to deal with these causal sequences when extracting attributions is to use a dotted line to mark a cause that is also an outcome. A second problem arises when a speaker clearly refers to a cause and an outcome, but these are separated by text or, as in the following example, by a second cause: *if you smack her [(4) because you've had enough of her defying you and telling you like] she'll say 'I don't love you, I'm going to run away' /*. Here the convention we have adopted is to place brackets around the text that is not being extracted as the first causal attribution. In this instance the two attributions would be listed as: (3) *if you smack her → she'll say 'I don't love you, I'm going to run away' /* and: (4) *you smack her ← because you've had enough of her defying you and telling you like /*.

(1) *If you smack Karen, → that just makes the problem worse /*

(2) *When she's naughty → she'll defy you all the way and she won't give in /*

(3) *if you smack her → she'll say 'I don't love you, I'm going to run away' /*

(4) *you smack her ← because you've had enough of her defying you and telling you like*

(5) *Well all kids say things like that → so you take them in your stride /*

(6) *if she carries on to the extent that → you have to give her a smack /*

(7) */ you have to give her a smack ← 'cos she's really getting defiant here*

(8) *you have to give her a smack → she'll sit and scream and carry on and things like that /*

(9) *She'll throw herself into a tantrum so much → that you feel like strangling her /*

(10) */ you have to give her a cuddle ← because she can't understand that when she's naughty and you're upset you can't cuddle her*

(11) */ 'Cos I put her into bed once ← with her being misbehaved*

(12) */ I couldn't do it no more ← 'cos she wrecked the bedroom*

(13)   *And all I could do was hear her screaming and carrying on.* →
       And it made me feel like going up and really smacking her hard /
(14)   *it made me feel like going up and really smacking her hard* → *So*
       now I can't do that /

Practise examples:

Stable–unstable

(1)   'My teachers couldn't believe it, *it was so unlike me to fail an*
      exam like that.'
      Unstable—the speaker is implying that failing the exam
      was an unusual occurrence and unlikely to occur again.
(2)   'I used to go out all the time. *I think it was just a phase of*
      growing up.'
      Unstable—the speaker refers to a 'phase' implying that the
      cause no-longer applies to current outcomes.
(3)   'I wasn't all that surprised at the result, *I've never been all that*
      good at chemistry.'
      Stable—although the outcome may be a one-off event, the
      cause—not being good at chemistry—is ongoing.
(4)   '*My teacher left halfway through the year* which made things
      difficult.'
      Unstable—the cause (a teacher leaving halfway through
      term) is unlikely to recur, there is also no evidence to sug-
      gest that the speaker believes the cause likely to have an
      ongoing influence.
(5)   'She helped me get the job *because she thought I had potential.*'
      This is an attribution where it would be worth returning to
      the text to check for additional information to decide whether
      the cause should be coded stable or unstable. It is not entirely
      clear whether the cause (someone thinking that the speaker
      has potential) has ongoing consequences for the speaker. As
      an isolated attribution where there is no additional informa-
      tion, the best strategy would be to code 'uncertain'.
(6)   'Jane has really changed *since she went to assertiveness classes.*'
      Stable—the cause (going to assertiveness classes) is per-
      ceived by the speaker to have had a relatively permanent

effect upon Jane and is therefore likely to have ongoing consequences in future.

Global–specific

(1) *'Hitchhiking through Australia made me really question whether I wanted to work for a large organisation.'*
Global—the speaker considers that her experience has had a long-term impact upon her choice of career (for this research, a global cause was defined as one that could potentially influence career decisions and outcomes).

(2) *'I got the lead in the play because of all the hard work I put in.'*
Specific—there is no evidence to suggest that this cause (putting in hard work) will have an impact on other outcomes related to work.

(3) *'They elected me captain because they thought I could do the job.'*
Specific—although the cause of this attribution could be interpreted by the coder as referring to 'competence' and, as such, having a potential influence on future work performance, there is not enough evidence for us to be able to code this attribution 'global' with confidence.

(4) *'Being a school representative meant that I had to meet quite a few different people.'*
Specific—there is no evidence to suggest that the cause has influenced a range of other non-trivial work outcomes.

(5) *'Unfortunately my first year grades weren't too good, I suppose I'd spent too much time getting involved in sports.'*
Specific—no evidence to suggest that the speaker considers the cause to have had wider consequences.

(6) *'I spent the summer working for another law firm, it gave me an invaluable insight into how the profession works.'*
Global—the cause could reasonably be assumed to have had an influence on career choice.

Internal–external

(1) *'My father suggested that I try for law.'*
Speaker / Target—External
Agent (father)—Internal

The cause (a suggested course of action) originates with the father of the speaker.

(2) *'The course appealed to me because it had a large practical component.'*
Speaker / Agent / Target (all same in this attribution)— External.
The cause of the appeal to the speaker is the practical component associated with taking this course.

(3) *'They decided to give me the job because I'd had so much experience.'*
Speaker / Agent—Internal
Target—External
The cause in this attribution is the speaker's level of experience and therefore internal to the speaker. The cause is coded external to the target (the recruiting company).

(4) *(How come you were asked to go to France?)* *'I just happened to be in the right place at the right time.'*
Speaker / Agent / Target (all same in this attribution as no other entity is specifically mentioned)—External
The attribution is coded external as the cause is considered situational by the speaker (i.e. being in the right place at the right time).

(5) *'I managed to persuade the team to change strategy, but it required a special effort.'*
Speaker / Agent—Internal
Target (team)—External
The attribution is coded internal to the speaker because the outcome (persuading the team) is a consequence of her actions. The cause would be considered external to the team.

(6) *'It was a wonderful opportunity because it meant that we could all travel to America.'*
Speaker / Agent / Target—External
Although the speaker refers to 'we' in this attribution, as no other party is specifically mentioned or distinguished, the convention is to code the speaker only. The attribution would be coded external as there is no evidence that the outcome originated as a consequence of the speaker's actions.

Personal–universal

(1) *'I reckon that I'm suited to a job which involves travel <u>because</u>
     <u>I've done so much travelling in the past.</u>'*
     Speaker / Agent / Target (all same)—Personal
     Personal—the speaker is attempting to portray herself as
     different from her fellow applicants.

(2) *'He was nervous about <u>getting into the water</u>, so I did what
     anybody would do, I talked him through and helped him to relax.'*
     Speaker / Target—Universal
     Agent (friend)—Personal
     Universal for speaker because he is presenting his actions
     as no different from what other people might do in his
     situation. Personal for agent, because the cause (fear of
     water) can be viewed as being a characteristic that is rela-
     tively unique.

(3) *(Why were you chosen?) '<u>I guess that my interest in Science</u>
     <u>Fiction made me a little different from the rest of the group.</u>'*
     Speaker / Agent / Target—Personal
     The cause in this attribution is the speaker's perceived dif-
     ference from the rest of the group.

(4) *'I decided to study Physics because <u>my 'A' Level teacher was</u>
     <u>really good at making the subject interesting.</u>'*
     Speaker / Target—Universal
     Agent (teacher)—Personal
     The cause of the choice to study physics is universal to the
     speaker, but personal to her teacher, because she is described
     in a way that would distinguish her from other people.

(5) *'I realised too late that <u>I didn't really know enough about the</u>
     <u>subject</u>, so I had to carry on.'*
     Speaker / Agent / Target—Uncertain
     There is not enough information in this attribution for one
     to make a confident decision about coding. In this situation
     the best strategy would be to code 'uncertain'.

(6) *'My friends think I'm a little strange <u>because I enjoy studying.</u>'*
     Speaker / Agent—Personal
     Target (friends)—Universal
     The speaker is attempting to distinguish himself from the
     group.

Controllable (1), uncontrollable (0)

(1) 'I decided to join the orchestra <u>because it meant that I could</u>
     <u>practise with other people.</u>'
     Speaker / Agent / Target—Controllable
     The speaker could reasonably have been expected to influ-
     ence the decision to join the orchestra.

(2) '<u>My friend persuaded</u> me to apply for the position.'
     Speaker / Target—Controllable
     Agent (friend)—Controllable
     Both the speaker and the agent in this attribution appear to
     have had influence over the decision to apply for the pos-
     ition. Although the initial persuasion comes from the friend
     (agent) the speaker could reasonably have been expected to
     not apply for the position if she had so wished.

(3) '<u>Everyone was so enthusiastic</u> I felt that I was being pushed into
     the decision.'
     Speaker / Target—Uncontrollable
     Agent (family)—Controllable
     Here the attribution is coded uncontrollable for the speaker
     as he implies that he has been 'pushed' into the decision.
     The attribution is coded controllable for the agent as they
     (family) are perceived by the speaker as forcing him into
     the decision.

(4) '<u>I got all the books I could on the subject</u> so that I would be really
     prepared.'
     Speaker / Agent / Target—Controllable
     The speaker implies that she influenced the outcome.

(5) 'In the end the elections didn't go so well, <u>because the printers</u>
     <u>were too late delivering the leaflets.</u>'
     Speaker / Target—Uncontrollable
     Agent (printers)—Controllable
     Although there is no definitive information in this attribu-
     tion that the agent (the printers) were able to influence the
     outcome, the speaker implies that they are to blame and
     therefore the attribution would be coded controllable for
     the agent. It is coded uncontrollable for the speaker as he
     gives no indication that he would have been able to influ-
     ence either the cause or the outcome.

(6) *'I've always enjoyed history <u>because my aunt works in the local</u>*
<u>museum.</u>'
Speaker / Target—Controllable
Agent—Controllable
This attribution is coded controllable for both speaker and
agent, because one might reasonably assume that both
could have influenced the outcome if they had so wished.

3

Attributions in clinical settings

In this chapter we explore the relevance of attributions in clinical settings. We describe key areas in which attribution theory has informed clinical practice and research. In the second part of the chapter, we describe how we have used the Leeds Attributional Coding System (LACS) to detect and modify causal beliefs. We have included some case material to show how clinical practitioners and researchers have used the LACS.

Clinical psychologists, psychiatrists and counsellors have long been interested in the way people make sense of events in their lives. Understanding how people arrive at explanations for their experiences can help unravel the causes of psychological and emotional distress. As we described in Chapter 1, cognitive-behavioural interpretations of human behaviour in which internal mental models determine emotional and behavioural reactions have proved very influential. In particular, research has shown that the attributions that individuals make for events, can predict subsequent emotional reactions. For example, a spouse might attribute her partner's aggression to pressures at work, or a failure on her own part to be sufficiently understanding. Each of these attributions may affect the way in which the spouse feels about her partner's aggression and her own subsequent response. Consistent maladaptive patterns of attributions can, over time, serve to exacerbate levels of distress or dysfunction. Consequently, detailed explorations of how individuals explain outcomes can provide insight into what are often complex problems. It can also help clinicians to identify effective interventions.

ATTRIBUTIONS AND DEPRESSION

The application of attribution theory to clinical research has probably been most widespread in the treatment of depression. Research has shown consistently how causal attributions can play an important role in the aetiology of depression. As we noted in Chapter 1, Martin Seligman has explored the association between attributions and depression. Seligman found that dogs failed to learn how to avoid electrical shocks when experimental conditions introduced a previously unknown means of escape. He labelled this phenomenon 'learned helplessness'. Once the dogs had learned that there was no escape, they were less likely to change their behaviour once escape was possible. Seligman argued that the same phenomenon was also typical of people who experienced depression. He proposed that people suffering from depression perceive all potentially negative events as uncontrollable. Consequently, depressives typically assume that no action on their part can alter the likelihood of similarly unpleasant events recurring. The assumption that they will experience unpleasant events almost at random causes depressives to feel helpless about their current situation, and hopeless about the future.

In a further development, Abramson, Seligman and Teasdale (1978) proposed that depression does not arise simply from a belief that negative events are uncontrollable. Depression, they suggested, occurs because of the type of attributions that an individual makes for those events. Furthermore, they claimed that people attributing unpleasant events to *internal, stable* and *global* causes were at a higher risk for developing depression. This pattern of attributions became known as the depressive attributional style. Consider the example of an adolescent boy being bullied at school. He may attribute the bullying to his being somehow different (*I'm not very good at socialising*). He may also attribute it to not being able to cope with his peer group (*I give in because I can't cope with hassle*). We can characterise the causes in both attributions as internal (a personality trait), stable (unchangeable) and global (potentially influential in many situations). This tendency to make internal, stable and global attributions may mean that the boy is less likely to do anything to avoid the bullying. He believes that something inside him, that is un-likely to change, has caused it. Consequently the boy is vulner-able to feelings of learned helplessness and possibly depression. In contrast, a boy who attributes bullying to causes that are external, unstable and specific may be less likely to experience helplessness. An example of such an attribution might be *it's only because they're jealous I made the football team.* As a result, he may be more proactive in attempts to stop or avoid the bullying.

Chris Brewin (1985) has questioned whether attributions cause depression (a vulnerability model), or whether they are a consequence of depression (a symptom model). Recent research appears to support a 'mixed aetiology' model. Evidence sug-gests that either a severely stressful event or an existing attribu-tional style may cause depression. Both can act independently to cause depression (Parry & Brewin, 1988). A depressive attribu-tional style may maintain depression through self-blame and feelings of hopelessness regarding the future. The most recent work in this field has focused on the 'hopelessness model' of depression. This model specifies a chain of distal and proximal causes resulting in a proximal sufficient cause of depression. Hopelessness is seen as a proximal sufficient cause. Hopeless-ness is the expectation that highly desired outcomes are unlikely to occur, or that highly aversive outcomes are likely to occur and that one is unable to influence this. However, hopelessness (and the attributions that characterises it) may not underlie all cases of depression. Clinical depression is a heterogeneous phenom-enon that may be caused by many different factors.

ATTRIBUTIONS AND DISTRESSED ADULT RELATIONSHIPS

Harold Kelley was the first to identify causal attributions as an important predictor of satisfaction with close relationships. He noted that people often speculate about the causes of events influencing their relationships. For example, couples frequently think about reasons for each other's hurtful or supportive be-haviour, why their sexual relationship has particular characteris-tics, or how the influence brought to bear by members of their extended family has developed. Since the late 1970s, research concerned with the role played by attributions in close adult relationships has grown rapidly. Consistent evidence supports the view that attributions not only act as moderators of relationship distress, but can also predict the long-term success of a relationship.

As Kelley suggested, people in relationships often make attributions. However, couples produce attributions with greater frequency during particular periods in a relationship. For example, people are more likely to make attributions about each other's behaviour at the beginning of a relationship. Most partner behaviour seems novel at the beginning of a relationship. Similarly, they will generate attributions during and after interpersonal conflict, when relationships are experiencing more long-term difficulty, and at the end of relationships. Evidence also suggests that women produce more attributions than men for relationship events when they perceive the relationship as satisfactory. However, once they encounter difficulties, men make as many attributions as women (Holtzworth-Munroe & Jacobsen, 1985). Consequently, it has been suggested that attributions produced by men rather than women might prove a better indicator of the state of a relationship. Men, it seems, are only prompted to search for the causes of relationship events when they sense difficulties.

Research concerning attributional activity in heterosexual relationships was important for a second reason. A key aim was to establish whether couples in distressed relationships made different types of attributions for similar relationship events compared with other couples. Results suggested that individuals in distressed relationships who were attending marital therapy tended to externalise responsibility for negative events. They attributed the cause instead to something internal to their partners. For example, someone in a distressed relationship might come up with an attribution such as 'We're always arguing because he refuses to help around the house'. Similarly, positive partner behaviour in distressed relationships was more likely to be attributed to external, unstable and specific causes (e.g. He only bought me flowers because his mother reminded him that it was my birthday). Researchers have described this pattern of attributing as distress-maintaining, because it focuses attention on negative outcomes and reduces attention on positive outcomes.

In contrast, individuals in successful, non-distressed relationships were more likely to accept personal responsibility for negative outcomes (e.g. *I suppose I shouldn't have taken the car without letting her know. She did have some reason to be annoyed*). Similarly, they tended to attribute their partner's negative behaviour to more external, unstable or specific causes. For example, *She's been experiencing quite a lot of pressure at work recently, it's making things difficult at home.* Positive partner behaviour, however, was attributed to causes internal to the partner, stable and global (e.g. *I have to do a lot of travelling for work. She's very supportive, particularly when it means that she has to look after the children by herself*). Holtzworth-Munroe & Jacobsen (1985) described this pattern of attributions as relationship-enhancing, in that it focuses attention on positive events, and reduces the affective impact of negative ones.

More recently, Frank Fincham and his colleagues have been particularly influential in this area. They have investigated the role of cognitions in marital satisfaction and marital therapy (see Fincham, Fernandes & Humphreys, 1993, for a review). Research has provided good evidence for the role of cognitions in understanding marital satisfaction. Partners in unhappy relationships make attributions emphasising negative marital events, rather than positive marital events. Evidence also suggests that couples in harmonious relationships have a much more variable pattern of attributing causes to marital events. It is as though we might characterise marital discord by couples consistently employing the same negative pattern of attributing. Interestingly, couples who believe they are very similar in their beliefs tend to be happier, although in reality their belief systems are not as similar as they would like to think. Without doubt cognitions, and attributions in particular, can be useful predictors of marital behaviour and, specifically, marital satisfaction.

The evidence for the effectiveness of cognitive marital therapy interventions is less convincing. Research shows that standard behavioural marital therapy (BMT) is just as effective. However, Fincham (1994) has suggested that we should not take this as evidence that cognitive variables do not play an important role in marital therapy. He has claimed that the problem may lie in treating cognitive interventions as an approach quite distinct from BMT. A more effective approach might be to identify the role that cognitions, and attributions, may play at different points in a range of different therapies. This change may involve rethinking the role of cognitions in marital therapy, focusing on processes rather than outcomes. The need for further longitudinal studies continues, but Fincham's work has provided intriguing insights into the relationship between attributional patterns and marital distress. Evidence is emerging that attributions can cause distress over time and are not merely reflections or symptoms of underlying difficulties in the relationship.

PARENTAL ATTRIBUTIONS FOR CHILDREN

Bell (1979) pointed out that most early research concerned with parent–child interactions overlooked the possibility that parents are motivated to make sense of children's behaviour. However, in recent years researchers and clinicians have paid increasing attention to the role of parental attributions. The way in which a parent explains a child's behaviour can influence the way in which the parent chooses to respond. For example, a parent may attribute the fact that her child has just spilt orange juice on the carpet to the child's tiredness. If so, she is less likely to feel angry with the child or use punitive measures. However, if a parent attributes the same outcome to the child's deliberate attempts to be spiteful (a seemingly extreme explanation, but one typical among abusive parents) she is much more likely to use punitive measures.

Daphne Bugental and her colleagues have pointed to the importance of parents' beliefs in their ability to exert control over their children. In most families, power and authority rests with parents. However, clinicians are all too aware that, in some families, parents perceive themselves to have no control over their children. In many of these families, parents typically describe their children as difficult. Paradoxically, this perceived lack of control is often associated with an increased likelihood of parents using more coercive and punitive strategies with their children.

Attributions may be particularly important in distressed and abusive parent–child relationships, and evidence suggests that abusive parents explain their children's behaviour (good and bad) in particular ways. For example, Larrance and Twentyman (1983) compared abusive with non-abusive or neglectful mothers. Physically abusive mothers were more likely to explain their child's misbehaviour in terms of internal and stable characteristics of the child such as 'a bad temperament' or 'a wilful personality'. That is, when their child misbehaved they were more likely to adopt strategies that only served to escalate conflict. Interesting parallels exist between these findings and the research concerned with close adult relationships. Parents who have difficult relationships with their children show similar attributional biases (minimising responsibility and externalising blame) shown by partners in distressed marital relationships. To date very little research has focused on the attributions made by children. This is an area that would appear ripe for further investigation and one that would lend itself ideally to the LACS methodology.

ATTRIBUTIONS AND THERAPEUTIC INTERVENTION

The research mentioned so far has potentially important implications for clinicians formulating therapeutic interventions. Focusing on the attributions individuals make can help clinicians understand how patients attempt to make sense of, and cope with, their own difficulties. An analysis of attributions can also help the clinician to select an appropriate intervention. Explaining their attributional style to patients can enable them to identify where they are falling foul of maladaptive cycles of explanations and negative effect. The following example comes from the clinic of the Leeds Family Therapy and Research Centre. We used the LACS with a man in his early twenties, whom his doctor had referred. The man had complained of recent, and increasingly frequent, aggressive outbursts towards people of whom he was fond. An assessment session identified that he had been beaten as a child by his father and mother, often for no apparent reason. Sometimes his father hauled him out of bed in the middle of the night, and hit him hard with no explanation. As a teenager he had felt very angry with his father. As he grew older, the man had frequently thought about hitting his father to pay him back for the childhood beatings. He had then become afraid that his feelings could lead to actions that he could not control. He worried he might literally kill his father if his father ever as much as 'laid a finger on him'.

To control his strong, angry feelings towards his father, the man had tried to be positive and friendly towards him or to ignore him. However, his thinking had become dominated by the idea that he could be an aggressive and dangerous person. Moreover, he was beginning to act on these feelings, becoming increasingly verbally aggressive. These verbal outbursts only served to confirm the view he held of himself as aggressive. Thoughts that he could kill his father if his father provoked him became increasingly intrusive. Since his father never stopped being aggressive towards him, the cycle continued. The man was afraid that a time would come when he could not control his impulses and angry outbursts towards others. By the time the man came to the clinic, he had a firm belief about himself as an aggressive person. However, he also had a striking contradiction in his thinking—namely that he was not aggressive. On listening to the man, he was clearly making attributions that were self-blaming, pessimistic and helpless. He perceived himself to be worthless and not liked by others. However, he was also aware that those around him were trying to tell him that they had a much more positive view of him. This man reacted against psychodynamic interpretations and insight into his behaviour. However, when we tape-recorded a therapy session and subsequently extracted and analysed his attributions, he became interested in working with his causal beliefs. After listening to his own interpretations of his situation, including the contradictory patterns of attributing, he became much easier to work with. Therapy progressed towards reframing the problem and developing more effective ways of dealing with the difficulties he faced.

Extracting and identifying attributions as part of therapy has also proved useful in some therapeutic interventions with rape victims. Janoff-Bulman and her colleagues studied attributions made by female victims of rape. They found that victims who

made what they described as characterological self-blame attributions (e.g. *There must be something about me which marked me
out*) recovered less well following the rape than women who
made behavioural self-blame attributions (e.g. *I should not have
walked down that passage, I knew it wasn't lit, I shouldn't have taken
the risk*). She argued that while all victims blamed the perpetrator, those who made self-blame attributions were attempting to
cope by striving for control over their situation. Victims who
thought that their rape was completely outside their control
found it especially difficult to cope with because, by implication,
it could occur again. Searching for some cause that they could
control, such as their own behaviour, victims were more likely
to conclude that they could probably avoid being raped in the
future. Janoff-Bulman pointed out, however, that encouraging
attributions in which the victim accepts even some small degree
of responsibility, could have potentially disastrous consequences for any legal action against the perpetrator. Characterological self-blame, on the other hand, is particularly
maladaptive. The attributions involved are akin to depressive
attributions, i.e. the victim blames, in part, some uncontrollable
and stable characteristic that he or she possesses. In such cases
the therapist may need to encourage the victim to relinquish
such a belief to help the individual to cope more effectively.

Results from other fields of interpersonal research might also
prove useful in the clinical domain. For example, attributional
bias shown by interviewers when assessing candidates for selection has been a popular topic within organisational research (see
Herriot, 1989). Quite simply, evidence suggests that interviewers, like most people, are vulnerable to bias in their perceptions of the causes of other people's behaviour. They are more
likely to attribute behaviour to internal characteristics of the
candidate and underestimate the role of situational factors. We
know this tendency as the fundamental attributional bias. Interviewers are also likely to make more favourable attributions for
members of a similar group as their own (in-group bias) and less
favourable attributions for those who belong to another group
(out-group bias). In the case of race and ethnicity, interviewers
can, quite unconsciously, engage in attributional biases that per-
petuate discrimination (Silvester & Chapman, 1996).

Clinical research has paid much less attention to biases that may influence the behaviour of practitioners. However, evidence suggests that bias does exist and can lead to differential decision making. Moreover, practitioners should be alerted to the possible influence of fundamental attributional bias in psychotherapy. Many forms of psychotherapy interpret unwanted or maladaptive behaviour shown by patients or clients as a symptom of some underlying dysfunction. Underlying dysfunctions may include personality disturbance, a deficiency in earlier attachments, or a well-established cognitive distortion. However, fundamental attributional error applied to diagnosis can lead to practitioners underestimating possible external causes of behaviour. Some researchers have claimed that over-representation of people from ethnic minorities in clinical populations may be the result of such a systematic bias.

One of the most consistent attributional errors we make has been described by Jones and Nisbett as the actor–observer bias. They argue that actors (i.e. people providing causes for their own behaviour) prefer explanations based on the circumstances in which they find themselves. Observers (people providing an explanation for the behaviour of another person) describe that behaviour as the product of some stable personality trait. Note that the claim is for tendencies. Jones and Nisbett are not suggesting that all attributions made by actors and observers will differ in this way. The experimental evidence in support of a systematic difference between the way actors and observers make attributions is quite strong. However, the question remains why this difference should occur. Jones and Nisbett claim that there are two reasons, both to do with the information that people use to arrive at a causal attribution. First, actors and observers do not have access to the same important information in forming beliefs about causes of behaviour. Observers rarely have information about:

- the emotional consequences of their behaviour for an actor;
- the circumstances in which an act took place;
- the intentions of the actor.

So, to summarize, actors and observers do not have access to the same information when making an attribution about the causes of an act. Observers have restricted data concerning the actors' experiences following the act. They also have restricted information about the circumstances in which an act takes place, including historical circumstances. Finally, they have very little information about the actor's intentions.

Second, actors and observers differ in the ways in which they use available information to arrive at an attribution. Jones and Nisbett have suggested that actors and observers put greater weight or importance on different bits of the information available to them:

- observers pay most attention to elements of a situation that are changing;
- observers assume their perceptions are objective, not subjective;
- observers will tend to focus on an actor's behaviour, not circumstances.

The whole issue of actor and observer differences begs the question about who is right, actor or observer? Evidence suggests that observers often get things wrong. Experiments have shown an unswerving readiness by observers to attribute an actor's behaviour to stable personality factors. Why should there be this tendency to overestimate the influence of personality factors and underestimate the impact of situational influences?

It is not just untrained lay observers who make this error. Psychologists have a long and chequered history of describing human behaviour as a collection of stable personality traits. Personality theorists have long claimed that we are born with certain genetically determined behavioural dispositions. In their view, behavioural dispositions are relatively immune to the influence of learning and experience.

According to Mischel (1973, p. 253), we can sum the trait approach to personality up using the following definition: '. . . *personality comprises broad underlying dispositions which pervasively influence the individual's behaviour across many situations and leads to consistency in his* [sic] *behaviour.'*

Given this assumption of behavioural consistency, the trait model of personality is empirically testable simply by observing behaviour over a variety of situations. Mischel summarises several studies that do just that. Consistency has been found to be high for behaviour associated with problem solving and intelligence. Consistency has also been evident when people are asked to rate their own behaviour, as with the common self-report questionnaire. Consistency across time has also been found when subjects are tested and retested in similar situations. However, when we monitor behaviour by a variety of techniques, for examples self-report questionnaires and observation, the evidence for consistency is much weaker. The evidence for stable personality traits does not hold up when we monitor behaviour across a variety of situations using different methods of assessment. Mischel (1968, p. 177) concludes: '*Individuals show far less cross-situational consistency in their behaviour than has been assumed by trait-state theories.*'

Why do we persist with beliefs in stable traits despite evidence to the contrary? We have already dealt with two of the reasons, i.e. restricted access to information and information-processing bias. Jones and Nisbett described three other biases:

- information bias—observers typically see actors in only a limited range of circumstances;
- information processing bias—the psychological need to see the world as controllable;
- language bias—we have many more words to describe personality compared with circumstances.

Finally comes the use of 'implicit personality theories'. These are the informal and untested theories that we tend to hold concerning patterns of traits and behaviours that go together. For example, 'fat people are happy' or 'quiet people are intelligent and reflective' are two popular implicit personality theories.

Once an observer has constructed and applied a personality to an actor, they can deal quite easily with any contradictory evidence that they may encounter. Given the large number of different personality labels available, finding one or more to confirm first impressions is not difficult. However, the tendency for observers to make this kind of error must be kept in perspective. The implications may be serious when psychologists fall prey to this distortion. However, does it really matter that, as observers, we make the same errors? Probably not. Without implicit personality theories, we would find dealing with people in social situations much more difficult due to the unpredictable nature of interactions.

To summarise, we have shown that when we make attributions about other people's behaviour we have a greater tendency to make dispositional (internal) attributions. When looking for causes for our own behaviour, we are much more likely to turn to situational factors.

Car driving is a good example of the phenomenon. If we see another driver jumping from one lane of traffic to another, we may label that person as competitive or aggressive. However, when we do the same, we justify it on the grounds of being in a hurry. Several reasons may account for this bias. We may have a great deal more in the way of historical information about our own behaviour. When observing others, this history is often unavailable. We make causal inferences solely on the grounds of observable behaviour. Similarly, it may be an attentional difference. Observers are drawn to look at an actor's overt behaviour and little else. When we seek causes for our own behaviour, we are drawn much more to the prevailing situation rather than thinking about the behaviour itself. The existence of this bias has several extremely important implications for our attitudes towards other people.

ATTRIBUTIONS MADE IN CLINICAL INTERVIEWS

In the following section we discuss three areas of our clinical work in which we have used the LACS to explore and understand attributions made by individuals. The first is an investigation into attributions made by mothers of young children suffering from non-organic failure to thrive (FTT). The second example illustrates how we used the LACS to monitor changes over time in attributions made by families in therapy. The final example describes an analysis of attributions produced by abusive families during diagnostic therapy sessions. It shows how these attributions relate to the decisions made by therapists regarding a likely prognosis for rehabilitation.

Attributions made by parents of children with non-organic failure to thrive

Failure to thrive occurs when an infant or child fails to achieve the expected growth as assessed by measurements of weight and height . . . it may result from feeding an infant inadequate calories or from a bizarre diet. (Hobbs, Hanks & Wynne, 1993)

Despite an abundance of cheap food, many children in wealthy western societies fail to thrive. For several years, researchers at the Leeds Family Therapy and Research Centre have been investigating parents' perceptions of the causes of failure to thrive. We have a substantial data set comprising the attributions mothers make for their children's eating behaviours. These attributions for eating behaviour have been made by mothers of children diagnosed as failing to thrive (non-organically), and by mothers whose children eat quite normally. Most of our work has been with mothers of infants who have yet to develop language. The examples presented draw on this data set to discuss insights that can be provided by a detailed analysis of attributions. The examples show how the attributional analyses influenced our clinical interventions with families. Like most work investigating parent–child relationships, a focus on mother–child relationships dominates this research. In FTT this reflects current social norms, i.e. mothers, rather than fathers, are more likely to be involved in the feeding of children. However, an investigation of fathers' attributions around feeding activities would be worth while in future.

Inevitably the actual causes of FTT are varied, as are the attributions that mothers produce for the causes of their children's failure to thrive. Often, however, attributions are an expression of a problem experienced within a family. Very often the problem involves dysfunctional parent–child interactions. The link between feeding and emotional care is important, as feeding often involves a child's first social relationship. Some psychologists have argued that establishing successful feeding behaviour between mother and child is essential to later development. Successful feeding relies on parents' sensitive reactions to a child's cues and, consequently, on parental interpretations of a child's needs.

Observations of mothers whose children are failing to thrive show a clearly identifiable lack of synchrony between mother and child during feeding interactions. For example, infants experiencing a new taste often react with facial expressions of dislike, spitting out the food, or looking away from the mother. Most mothers allow an infant time to become accustomed to a new taste. However, mothers of children with FTT often fail to allow sufficient time for their infants to adapt. They may try to force more food on their children before the infants are ready. Alternatively, they may decide prematurely that their children does not like the food and fail to persist with feeding. The way in which mothers explain their children's behaviour or needs can be crucial in determining how they respond. Over a series of feeds, a mismatch between the child's needs and the mother's interpretation of those needs can occur. The result can be extremely distressed and asynchronous interactions. A child who is not receiving sufficient nourishment, particularly if this is associated with tense, difficult and sometimes painful episodes, can become distressed at the sight of food. This distress may prevent the child from taking any subsequent food effectively. A mother will frequently get upset when faced with her child's distress, resulting in the whole feeding interaction spiralling into increasing chaos.

Interviews with mothers

Interviews were conducted with mothers of children who had already been diagnosed as suffering from failure to thrive. We were interested in exploring the attributions mothers held concerning why their children had been diagnosed as FTT, and how they perceived their families' eating habits overall. Researchers taped and subsequently transcribed interviews verbatim. They then extracted attributions and coded them using the LACS. Consistent with other clinical research, mothers made attributions at a rate of approximately one attribution per minute. Analysis of the attributions revealed complex, idiosyncratic patterns made by mothers in different families. However, some patterns of causal beliefs emerged which were typical of certain groups of mothers. What follows are descriptions of four different patterns, and examples of attributions made by the mothers concerned.

The first pattern of attributions uncovered were those in which mothers attributed FTT to causes located within their children, but over which the children have no control. The following is an example of such an attribution: *'She can't chew food properly, she's only just turned two.'* This attribution is coded 'unstable' on the assumption that the mother believes that this situation will change as the child gets older. *'She doesn't eat because she's not well.'* We code this as a 'global' attribution because it suggests that the child not being well influences outcomes other than eating. *'When he doesn't eat it's because he's not hungry.'* We code this as 'specific', making the link between being hungry and eating but not extending it to any other reason. Sturm and Drotar (1989) found that most parents attributed FTT to illness on the part of their children, rather than to environmental causes. This may be a defensive reaction by the parents. Accepting that a child is failing to thrive because of an uncontrollable biological factor rather than an inadequate diet may be easier for a parent.

Clinical interviews suggest that mothers of children who fail to thrive have a greater tendency to attribute events to causes that are global, stable, external and uncontrollable. Mothers see that they have difficulties in coping with stressful situations. This is particularly so when they see no end to the causes of those situations (stable) and when they believe the same causes to have wide-reaching consequences (global). Children who are failing to thrive generally look thin, may be moody, are more prone to illness, and do not sleep. The fact that mothers may have failed to establish adequate feeding routines can result in many perceiving the situation to be beyond their control. Mothers whose children show no symptoms of FTT do attribute some aspects of their children's behaviour to causes they believe to be uncontrollable. However, compared with mothers of FTT children, they make uncontrollable attributions much less frequently.

We can characterise the second pattern as a depressive attributional style. Some mothers of children who fail to thrive express causal beliefs associated with feelings of helplessness and depression. In depressive patterns of attributing, people often express beliefs about the causes of unpleasant events being lodged within themselves. For example, *'It feels as if I am not feeding her because I am going through such a lot.'* Similarly, mothers frequently blame themselves for their children's condition, but believe they have little control over it, as the following attribution illustrates: *' I haven't got the energy as to what she eats I don't care what she eats or doesn't'*. Clinical interventions with mothers who have such an attributional style need to be thought through carefully. We have found that encouraging feelings of responsibility and personal involvement without also encouraging beliefs about control can sometimes reinforce depression. Monitoring the attributions of such mothers for a depressive pattern (stable, personal, uncontrollable attributions) is evidently important.

One mother talked of her own quite desperate need to stay thin. She dissolved into tears when we suggested she relax a rule forbidding her under-nourished child biscuits, crisps and chocolate to help her put on weight. The mother said: *'I don't know why you are worried about my daughter's weight. She is fine, there is nothing wrong with her.'* We explained why we were concerned, showing her a weight chart and establishing her child's weight as significantly below average. Her response was: *'She can't have those things. We have a rule that they do not come into the house.'* Asked whether she could explain to us how that rule had come about, she made the following attributions: *'My husband teases me that I am fat because I eat such things. And if they are in the house I will eat them as well, I can't resist. If I eat them I will be fat again'*. Recognising the attributional pattern, we knew we had to be careful not to propel the mother into a depressive state. However, at the same time we needed to act quickly to help the child put on weight. Our clinical intervention considered our understanding of the woman's causal beliefs.

The third pattern among mothers with FTT children concerned attributions for body size. The fact that people are easily tempted to pursue fashions is no surprise. We accept as part of modern life in Western cultures that this includes dieting. The desire to be thin can, for some people, particularly young women (but also boys), provoke serious illness. Anorexia nervosa and bulimia are at the extreme end of this continuum. People's desires to be thin affect many families. Often, obsessive eating behaviours have at their root misperceptions about body shape. Mothers can have a powerful effect when they apply attitudes about food to beliefs concerning the size and shape of children in a family.

Many mothers interviewed as part of our research had difficulties in accepting that the needs of young children may be very different from their own. A slimming diet that may be acceptable for an adult would not be acceptable for a growing child. McCann, Stein, Fairburn and Dunger (1994) found that many mothers with FTT children admitted to deliberately trying to make their babies more slim. Despite being aware of the diagnosis of failure to thrive, over half the mothers in the sample still believed their children to be of normal weight or just underweight. In addition, a similar proportion of mothers restricted their (underweight) children's intake of sweet foods and other foods with fat calorie and content (like fried foods, meat, nuts and biscuits) because they considered these unhealthy.

The fourth and final pattern concerned attributions made by mothers concerning their own behaviour. In the attribution 'If I got to rush off somewhere, I give up trying to feed him' the mother concerned takes responsibility for what is happening. Consequently, we code the attribution as 'internal'. In the next example, 'I hate cooking, so I do the easy meals', we code the attribution as 'personal'. The speaker is inferring that to hate cooking is a personal characteristic, not one the mother believes all mothers would hold.

One frequently voiced complaint from mothers is that 'I don't get any sleep because my child is constantly hungry and wants feeding even in the night'. The mother of a 2-year-old child made this comment. Her views reflected a popular belief that feeding children other than at mealtimes was unacceptable. What this mother's belief also indicated was that she thought she had no control over the matter and that the situation was unlikely to change. Consequently, the woman found the situation quite stressful. The child's weight had fallen to the point at which we needed to take swift action. We discussed the mother's predicament with her and suggested that she continued to feed her child at night. We predicted that the child would put on weight and that the sleepless nights would soon be a thing of the past. We agreed to share the responsibility with her over the prediction that she would spoil the child and it would demand food at night forever. As predicted, regular feeding night and day resulted in the child showing a considerable increase in weight the next time we saw the family. This example shows how patterns of 'uncontrollable' beliefs in conjunction with 'stable' beliefs can lead to dysfunctional interactions with mothers in this position. In this case, it resulted in a lack of flexibility detrimental to the child.

Mothers of children whose physical development is not a concern often attribute difficulties with their children's behaviour to unstable causes. The belief that problems will only be temporary can make problem situations more bearable and help mothers to manage.

Attributions and family therapy sessions

We originally developed the LACS as a method for exploring in detail the attributions produced by families during family therapy sessions. The way in which families explained events involving different family members has given us some powerful insights into the systemic relationships within the family.

The Leeds Family Therapy and Research Centre (LFTRC) has, over several years, provided family therapy in a research setting. Facilities enabling us to record therapy sessions on video and subsequently transcribe them has created a sizeable archive. One purpose to which we have put this archive is to investigate the role of attributions in family interactions. As discussed earlier in this chapter, several theoretical models have suggested relationships between causal beliefs and expressed emotion. The most widely investigated of these theoretical models is probably the learned helplessness model of depression proposed by Martin Seligman and his colleagues. However, the learned helplessness model has little to say concerning family functioning or the role of attributions in other emotional disorders.

The development of the LACS provided researchers at the LFTRC with the means to examine causal beliefs expressed in therapy. In particular, we have examined whether specific patterns of attributions might be associated with different aspects of family functioning. We began by looking at three key issues:

1. Do members of families in therapy have shared beliefs about the causes of unpleasant events that are systematically different from shared beliefs expressed by families not in therapy?
2. Do families in therapy adopt a consistent view concerning the causes of unpleasant events, i.e. do they have an attributional style to account for unpleasant events?
3. If a consistent attributional style was found among families in therapy, how might such a style influence the families' ability to cope with the consequences of unpleasant events. What are the implications for formulating clinical interventions with such families?

Comparisons between families attending the LFTRC for therapy and families recruited from the local community did provide some evidence of differences in patterns of attributing. Families in therapy had a greater tendency to make attributions for the unpleasant events they experienced to stable and global causes. Families in therapy tend to see the sources of their problems as relatively permanent; they are also more likely to view the same causes as having a malevolent influence on other areas of their lives. One might sum up these attributional tendencies as pessimism: families in therapy believe things are bad, they are not going to improve, and because other situations might be adversely influenced as a result, things are likely to get worse.

Other differences were found concerning the internal–external and personal–universal dimensions. Families in therapy were more likely to make attributions involving causes that were both internal and personal. Researchers have interpreted this combination of internal and personal attributions as a trait-based explanation as opposed to a situational explanation. The evidence suggests that families in therapy are more likely to attribute their problems to some unique trait or characteristic they possess, rather than circumstances. Such a view can often be maladaptive when it comes to coping with adverse events. Research has suggested that people often protect their self-esteem by consistently making trait attributions for success, but circumstantial attributions for failure. Although these attributions may not reflect reality very accurately, they do serve to protect one's self-esteem. Depressed people may have a more accurate view of the extent to which they are responsible for their misfortune, but it does not make them any happier.

Finally, the tendency of families in therapy to come up with trait-based explanations for unpleasant or negative events was not restricted to those providing explanations for their own behaviour. Where we asked that people speculate about the causes of problems experienced by other family members, they tended to offer similar explanations. The consequences of these tendencies for family members to make attributions likely to impair self-esteem is interesting in the context of therapy. It is as though families in therapy have developed a style of attributing that reinforces and perpetuates a cycle of despair and pessimism. For the therapist, these beliefs about causality are likely to mitigate against attempts to work with the family to shift their pessimistic views.

We can summarise the evidence concerning our three key issues thus: We have found some evidence of systematic differences between patterns of attributions made by families in therapy and matched controls. Our findings suggest that analysis of attributions might offer clinicians some useful insights when formulating interventions in family therapy contexts. For example, the pessimistic pattern of attributing unpleasant events to stable and global causes is evidently consistent with families having low expectations for their future. Therapists working with families who view causality in this way might formulate interventions designed to shift attributions towards causes that are more specific and unstable. However, a more realistic goal of therapy might be to encourage the minimum degree of change, to free clients to find their own solutions in future. If it is the combination of stable and global beliefs that is crucial, then targeting just one dimension for change could cause the desired effect.

A similar approach to shifting attributions from the internal and personal combination may be useful. Families in therapy have a tendency to use trait explanations for unpleasant events.

Other families we have studied also make attributions involving causes rated as personal, although causes rated as both personal and internal tend to be less common. We acknowledge that unpleasant events may happen due to some idiosyncratic features of the actors involved. However, therapeutic interventions might aim to explore the extent to which circumstances also play a role.

Finally, our experience suggests that families may get into perpetuating cycles of reinforcing maladaptive attributions by providing trait explanations for each other's behaviour. Such cycles can depress self-esteem, restricting the ability of families to cope with adverse circumstances. Ultimately this can make it more difficult for therapeutic interventions to bring about change. In such circumstances, clinical interventions might aim to reduce blame in such families, so enabling family members to develop greater self-esteem.

Thus far, we had established the existence of an association between maladaptive patterns of attributions and family relationships. The next stage was to look at whether changes in patterns of attributions were evident within families over therapy. From archive material held by the LFTRC on more than 40 families, therapists were asked to rate on a five-point scale 'the degree of positive change you feel [the family] have exhibited over the course of therapy'. We identified the five families rated most consistently by all six therapists as having undergone the most positive change. We also selected the five families rated most consistently as not having undergone any positive change. For each of these 10 families, we transcribed their first and final therapy sessions, and extracted and coded attributions according to the LACS method. The aim of the study was to identify patterns of attributions evident within families, and to look for evidence of change in those patterns during therapy. We predicted that the greatest change in patterns of attributing would be found in those families rated as having undergone the most change by therapists.

Evidence from this small number of families was mixed. We found only very few systematic differences between the two groups of families. The first concerned attributions rated on the stable–unstable dimension. Families rated by therapists as not having changed during therapy had a tendency to perceive the causes of their difficulties as more stable in nature compared with the other group of families. Attributional differences on this dimension may be evident before therapy begins. Families more resistant to change appear to have more entrenched beliefs about the extent to which the causes of their problems are immutable. Family therapy, it would appear, has little impact on these particular causal beliefs.

A further finding concerned the extent to which family members used trait or personality explanations for each other's, rather than their own, problem behaviours. Compared with first therapy sessions, all families—the 'change' and 'no change' groups—tended to use more trait explanations in their final session. As discussed earlier, trait explanations for unpleasant events have been associated with low self-esteem, and have consequently been labelled as maladaptive. That both groups of families showed the same increased tendency to use such explanations during therapy is puzzling. How could families rated as having undergone positive change be blaming each other for family problems to a greater extent? One possible explanation concerns the use of trait explanations in conjunction with stable attributions. Perhaps trait explanations are less maladaptive if the traits invoked are perceived as changeable. Families rated as having changed may have believed that each other's personal characteristics was a source of difficulty, but nonetheless saw those characteristics as open to change.

However we might wish to speculate, the fact remained that we failed to find any consistent changes in patterns of attributing over the course of therapy. The lack of change was evident in all families, irrespective of whether therapists rated them as having undergone positive change during therapy. At least, for this small group of families, clinical change was not associated in any systematic way with attributional change. Our results may not preclude the possibility that individual families changed their beliefs about causality in different ways during therapy. However, they are inconsistent with the idea that clinical change is somehow synonymous with attributional change.

Attributions produced by abusive parents

The final area in which we have used the LACS draws on work carried out with Arnon Bentovim at Great Ormond Street Hospital. We report this work more fully in Silvester, Bentovim, Stratton and Hanks (1995). The research addressed the question of whether attributions produced by abusive families during diagnostic therapy sessions might act as indicators of dysfunction. Evidence suggested that therapists might use these attributions, at least in part, to guide the decisions they make regarding a family's likely prognosis for rehabilitation.

The legal courts and social services refer families to the Department of Psychological Medicine at the hospital. Clinicians assess them regarding their likely benefit from further intervention and help. Some families are so actively opposed to help that it is in the abused child's best interests that he or she be removed from the family. In such circumstances, clinicians argue that no amount of help can realistically improve the situation for the child. Resources would be better directed to those families who are more likely to benefit from help. The problem facing professionals involved in such decision making is: how to decide which families are likely to benefit and which not?

Remarkably little research has been directed at the questions of how professionals decide, or whether the criteria used to decide are valid. We conducted an exploration of whether patterns of attributions produced by parents during diagnostic therapy sessions might predict different ratings of the family by the therapists involved. More specifically, we suggested that those families rated as more severe, and therefore least likely to benefit from therapeutic intervention, would make attributions for negative outcomes (including the abuse) which were stable, global and which blamed the child. Families rated more likely to respond to rehabilitation would make more unstable and specific attributions. Parents would be more willing to accept at least some responsibility for the abuse.

To test these predictions, the therapists at Great Ormond Street divided 18 families into one of three categories: those that in their opinions had a 'Good' prognosis for rehabilitation following therapeutic intervention; those with an 'Average' likelihood of benefit; and, finally, those with a 'Poor' prognosis. The families were typical of the range of families presenting at the Centre, and also the range of dysfunction. The types of abuse included physical and sexual abuse, neglect, Munchausen Syndrome-by-Proxy, and abuse by a parent or someone outside the family. The diagnostic sessions with each of these families had already been videotaped with the permission of the families involved. The discourse from these videotapes was then transcribed verbatim and the attributions extracted and coded. Typical examples of the attributions produced by parents are as follows:

1.   *'He was born like that, I'm always going to worry.'*
2.   *'Her behaviour is putting the whole family at risk.'*
3.   *'We're at this interview because the social worker doesn't trust us.'*
4.   *'Most kids mess around when they're twelve, so I mean it (sexualised behaviour) is just interest rather than sexual excitement.'*
5.   *'It's just his nature, he doesn't realise that he can hurt someone.'*
6.   *'She (two-month-old infant) is doing that to annoy me.'*

The results of the study provided support for the argument that attributional patterns differentiated between the different groups of families. In families with a 'Good' prognosis, parents displayed a less severe polarisation in their perceptions of control for negative outcomes. They attributed less control to the abused child and more to themselves. These families also made more unstable attributions. Families with a 'Poor' prognosis, however, were typified by a much smaller frequency of attributions in total. They were simply less likely to talk about the child or their relationship with the child. This may represent a defensive stance. Families may have already had such a prolonged and unsatisfactory relationship with professionals that they are simply unwilling to engage or participate in the session. Alternatively, in these instances, the child is simply not a focus of interest for the parents and therefore not a focus for attributional activity. Certainly for these parents, more attributions were produced by the parents for themselves than the child.

While identifying general trends and patterns of attributions is important, abuse, like most other clinical problems, is clearly multifaceted. Indeed, clinicians can also gain important insights into a case by studying the unique patterns of attributions present. In the next section we discuss the patterns of attributions produced during the diagnostic therapy session by each of three different families. In each case the patterns of attributions have been presented in numerical form.

The father in this first family (Table 3.1), rated 'doubtful' by therapists as to their likely prognosis for rehabilitation, presents a typical pattern of attributions found in physically abusive families. The pattern is similar to that found by Fincham, Beach and Baucom (1987) in highly distressed adult relationships, labelled 'polarisation'. Before discussing this in more detail, we should explain the numbers. The attributions included here are all produced (spoken) by the father who, in this instance, we have identified as having physically abused his 7-year-old son. They are also attributions where either the father is discussing himself as the agent (cause) of negative outcomes, or when his son is the agent of negative outcomes. No positive attributions are included. This is because attributions for positive events are relatively rare in these interviews. To achieve comparability across different families, we have converted original numbers of attributions into percentages. These percentages represent the proportion of attributions produced by the father that were stable, global and so on. Thus we can see that in this example of a physically abusive father, he makes more stable, global,

TABLE 3.1   Pattern of attributing in a family suspected of physical abuse

	Agent	
	Father	Child
Stable	35.7	53.8
Global	50.0	76.9
Internal	64.3	92.3
Personal	42.9	92.3
Controllable	14.3	84.6
Number of attributions	14	13

internal, personal and controllable (by his son) attributions for negative events caused by the child when compared with events caused by himself.

This pattern of attributions is also similar to the 'distress-maintaining' pattern of attributions described by Holtzworth-Munroe and Jacobsen (1985). It shifts attention away from the father's involvement in negative outcomes, so reducing his responsibility and, instead, focusing blame upon the child. It is possible that this father is ensnared in a maladaptive cycle of attributing. It may reflect a need to protect his self-esteem which ultimately exacerbates difficulties in the relationship by focusing attention on child misbehaviour. Illustrative examples of the attributions he made include: '*He doesn't get books 'cos he'll only tear them up*' and '*He just spits out food; it makes me so mad*'. The task for any therapist working with this family might therefore be to refocus the father's attention upon his son's positive behaviours, while building his own self-esteem as a parent and helping him to accept responsibility for the abuse.

It may, however, be a little premature to claim that all forms of abuse and all abusive families display similar patterns of attributions. The mother in the next family (Table 3.2) had been diagnosed as presenting with Munchausen Syndrome-by-Proxy. She had repeatedly attempted to suffocate and poison her child, each time seeking medical help, claiming that the child was ill.

TABLE 3.2   Pattern of attributing in a family suspected of Munchausen Syndrome-by-Proxy

	Agent	
	Mother	Child
Stable	57.9	75.0
Global	63.2	62.5
Internal	89.5	100
Personal	63.2	62.5
Controllable	5.3	0
Number of attributions	19	8

The child was 2 years old at the time of the interview. As this was a single case of Munchausen Syndrome-by-Proxy, any generalisation must be made with extreme care. However, interesting differences between the attributions that this mother produced and those of other physically abusive parents were evident. Therapists categorised this family as 'hopeful' in that they considered there to be a reasonable probability of being able to promote positive change.

Again the attributions represent those where the mother discusses either herself or her child as causing a negative event. In contrast to the previous father, however, she appears to display a helpless and potentially depressive attributional pattern. She attributes negative outcomes to stable and global causes that are also internal and personal to herself, yet uncontrollable. There may be little of the externalising found in the father's pattern and, similarly, there is little indication of blame of the child. Indeed, this child is seen as having little control over the negative outcomes. In fact the pattern of attributions is more reminiscent of that found in certain of the mothers with children diagnosed as FTT. As with these mothers, the therapist's task might be to encourage the mother to adopt a more adaptive pattern of attributions and accept more responsibility, without risking exacerbating the depression that may already be present. Without further research, making a claim that we should treat parents demonstrating Munchausen Syndrome-by-Proxy differently from other abusive parents is difficult. However, the possibility would be worthy of future investigation.

In the final family (Table 3.3) the father has been identified as sexually abusing a 14-year-old stepdaughter. While he has admitted the abuse, the pattern of attributions that he reveals during the diagnostic therapy session is revealing. For this family, although the attributions are those spoken by the father, they are for outcomes where either he or the child are the target. For example, in the following attribution made by the father he is the target: *'There were no real alternatives, I had to take the night job.'* In the following attribution his daughter is the target: *'They were teasing her at school, so she went out and bought makeup.'*

TABLE 3.3   Pattern of attributing in a family suspected of sexual abuse

	Agent	
	Father	Child
Stable	57.1	0
Global	61.9	50.0
Internal	47.6	75.0
Personal	71.4	75.0
Controllable	19.0	50.0
Number of attributions	21	4

This pattern of attributing is interesting, because the father makes far more attributions where he is the target (victim?) than where his daughter is the target, despite the fact that she is the one who has been identified as having been sexually abused. Of these attributions, far more control is attributed to his daugher than he attributes to himself. This suggests that he is not accepting responsibility for these events. If therapists are to work successfully with this family they would need to address the issue of blame which still occurs, albeit more subtly in the form of attributions where father and daughter are the target rather than the agent of negative outcomes.

The study of spoken attributions produced by abusive parents offers a sensitive and ecologically valid strategy for assessing social cognitions in an extremely difficult area to research. The potential for further investigations of how patterns of attributions become shared by family members through discussion is considerable. Snyder and Higgins (1988) describe individuals as negotiating a 'shared reality' through talk. We predict that families achieve similar shared realities through talk (and argument). As Wells (1981) pointed out, causal attributions do not only arise when people witness events directly. People also adopt them through the secondary acquisition of attributions communicated to them by others for events that they did not witness. An understanding of how causal attributions contribute to the maintenance of distress in families would prove fascinating material for future studies.

However, we must offer a word of caution at this point. The study of spoken attributions generates a very rich source of data. Nevertheless, it is time-consuming and does not always conform to the rigours of more traditional empirical research. We would argue that in a research context both approaches need to progress hand in hand. A focus on actual attributions in discourse reminds the researcher of the sophistication of individuals engaged in causal reasoning. It can also provide an excellent starting point for further questionnaire and laboratory-based research. Secondly, as Edwards and Potter (1993) pointed out, we cannot assume that attributions are simply windows on the mind or direct reflections of underlying cognitions. However, the available evidence does warrant the conclusion that spoken attributions can never illustrate static underlying cognitions. However, their point is an important one. To progress further with investigations of spoken attributions, we need to clarify the additional factors that can contribute to spoken attributions beyond internal cognitions. Future work investigating attributions and distressed relationships needs somehow to incorporate recognition of the 'appropriateness' of certain attributional patterns. It also needs to examine the extent to which social presentation influences public attributions.

CONCLUSIONS

In this chapter, we have given the reader a basic introduction to the relevance of attributions in clinical settings. We have described key areas in which attribution theory has informed clinical practice and research. Using some examples of research done in the LFTRC, we hope to have shown the potential that attribution theory has for the clinical practitioner. A much more detailed analysis of the relationship between attribution theory and clinical practice can be found in Forsterling (1988), *Attribution Theory in Clinical Psychology*.

It would be a mistake to conclude that hypothesised relationships between causal beliefs and psychological functioning have been verified by sound empirical evidence. As yet, the efficacy of clinical interventions aimed at shifting causal beliefs remains unproved. However, the examples we have discussed suggest that continued research into the role attributions may play in the aetiology of cognitive functioning is warranted. In the experience of clinicians working at the LFTRC and elsewhere, analysis of attributions has provided some useful insights into problems brought into the clinic.

4

Attributions at work

This chapter is concerned with attributions that individuals produce in the workplace. It describes, using three case examples, how researchers and practitioners can use the LACS to explore the attributions people make in organisational settings. We aim to show how quantifying patterns of causal attributions can provide insight into the processes which contribute to organisational behaviour, decision making and change. The chapter begins with a consideration of why workplace attributions are an important topic for study. We will provide illustrative attributions taken from four levels of organisational activity.

WHY ARE WORKPLACE ATTRIBUTIONS IMPORTANT?

Simon is a graduate trainee. He has spent the past six months working in different sections of his new company and the experience has been a challenging one. Not only has he had to learn how to perform new tasks, he has also had to fit in with his new work colleagues. Simon has had to cope with the different management styles of each of his supervisors. He has also had to behave in a way which he thinks will enhance his future prosperity. In all this time Simon has been making causal attributions in an attempt to make sense of, and negotiate, his new environment. These attributions have included explanations for the behaviour of his colleagues, his managers and even his own actions. He has also listened to attributions made by senior people in the company, in an attempt to learn about why different organisational events occur. These attributions have helped Simon to decide how he should respond in each new situation that he encounters.

For example, during his placement with the finance department, Simon's supervisor commented that the tie Simon was wearing was particularly 'lively'. Simon thought about the comment and the tie, which he had only recently bought from a new and rather trendy store in town. Could the comment be a compliment? In which case should he continue to buy 'lively' ties in an attempt to make a good impression as a creative person? Alternatively, was his supervisor suggesting that the tie was out of place? One glance around the room at his colleagues quickly confirmed Simon's suspicions. The next day he, too, wore a blue tie. Simon had attributed his supervisor's comment to a recommendation that he should conform to an unofficial company uniform of grey suits and blue ties. He changed his behaviour accordingly.

Although this example may seem inconsequential, causal attributions are central to workplace behaviour and organisational functioning. They help individuals at all levels of organisational activity to identify the causes of new and potentially threatening situations. By doing so, people can make appropriate and effective responses. Consequently, attributions can have an important impact upon individual and organisational performance. We can think of workplace attributions occurring at each of four levels. First, at an individual level where people produce causal attributions for their own behaviour and events in which they are involved. Second, people produce causal attributions at an interpersonal level: these are attributions produced by one person when they explain another person's behaviour. Third, attributions are produced at an intergroup level. They include explanations produced by members of one group for outcomes associated with their own group or those of another group. Finally, attributions occur at an organisational level. We can define these as causal attributions for organisational events which members of that organisation share. The next section will explore how attributions at each of these levels relate to organisational behaviour. In the final section we will discuss how researchers and practitioners can use attributional coding to investigate causal beliefs further.

Attributions at an individual level

As we have already mentioned in this book, people are motivated to make attributions. Explaining their own behaviour and events that affect them helps people to render their environment more predictable and thus, potentially, more controllable. Such attributions can have a pertinent influence upon organisational behaviour. Let's take Susan, who works as a salesperson in a clothing store, as an example. Her manager has encouraged Susan to approach customers when they enter the store and offer them assistance. The store also operates a bonus system for those employees who sell the most clothes. While Susan is working, a young woman comes into the store with her partner and begins to look at a selection of evening dresses. Susan goes up to her and asks if she needs any assistance. The woman explains that she is going to a party at her partner's company and would like to wear something a little special. Susan tries to help her decide. She spends time chatting with the customer. However, while they discuss the different dresses, the woman's partner becomes restless and in the end they leave without buying anything.

Naturally Susan feels a little disheartened by her failure to sell what could have been a relatively expensive dress. The event triggers a process of attributional activity. Susan tries to explain what went wrong. In reality the sale may have been lost for several reasons. For example, it might be that the customer saw nothing that she liked. Alternatively, it may have been because the woman's partner was bored and wanted to leave. Susan could attribute it to her own failure to persuade the customer to try on the dresses. More generally, Susan may attribute the failure to her need for more training. Each of these attributions is likely to result in a different emotion. However, the cause Susan finally identifies as the most likely explanation can have important implications for how she responds to similar situations in future. For example, Bernard Weiner has argued that the type of causal attributions we make for successes and failures influence future reactions to similar situations. Specifically, whether we are more likely to give up or try harder in future achievement situations. In Susan's case, a lost sale attributed to the wrong sales strategy is more likely to result in Susan changing her behaviour. Behaviour change would be less likely if she attributed it to her own inadequacies as a salesperson, or the customer's behaviour. Put simply, if Susan believes the cause of the lost sale to be within her control, she is more likely to strive harder for success in future.

Work carried out by Martin Seligman in the United States has shown that individuals vary considerably in their attributional style. Someone's attributional style is the typical way in which they explain outcomes. He describes people as either 'optimists' or 'pessimists'. On the one hand, optimists tend to attribute positive outcomes to personal factors and negative outcomes to external factors or luck. On the other hand, pessimists typically attribute negative outcomes to personal factors like lack of ability. Similarly, they attribute positive outcomes to the behaviour of others or luck. We could describe Henry Ford as an optimist given his famous comment that 'failure is only the opportunity to begin again more successfully'. Ford believed that outcomes were within his personal control. He was not, in his view, simply at the mercy or whim of external forces.

Seligman also found that attributional style was particularly important for salespeople. For example, in a study of insurance agents he found that not only did optimists sell more insurance than pessimists, they also displayed lower levels of employee turnover. It seems that optimists were more resilient to the frequent failure situations that they encountered when trying to sell insurance and maintained a higher level of effort. Pessimists, however, became disheartened much more quickly and their level of effort declined. Attributional style has also been shown to act as an important moderator of reactions to redundancy and long-term unemployment. The causal attributions people make for why they became unemployed predict the extent to which they engage in subsequent job-seeking behaviour. Those with a more optimistic attributional style immediately following redundancy were more likely than those with a pessimistic attributional style to have found a new job six months later.

Attributions at an interpersonal level

Interpersonal attributions are causal attributions that one person makes for another person's behaviour. We are most likely to make attributions for another person's behaviour when that behaviour is relevant to us personally. For example, we may look for the causes of a friend's behaviour if he or she suddenly behaves unpleasantly towards us. In reality, interpersonal attributions usually occur with individual attributions. We can take the sales situation described above as an illustration of this. Following a failed sale, the sales-person is likely to look for causes that could be either internal (*I did not try hard enough, I'm not good enough*) or external. In the outcome of an interaction the external cause can be interpersonal, for ex-ample, 'the customer's partner was bored' or 'the customer proba-bly saw something she liked better elsewhere'.

In fact, salespeople will usually make interpersonal attributions during any interaction with customers in an attempt to determine the causes of their reluctance or enthusiasm concerning a particular product. Good salespeople can probably make accurate attribu-tions for customer reactions and consequently can adapt their own responses and maximise the likelihood of a successful sale. For example, a car salesperson may attribute a particular customer's lack of enthusiasm for power steering to a poor understanding of its advantages. Consequently, the salesperson may try to provide further information about how it can improve the quality of the customer's driving experience. Alternatively, if the lack of interest is attributed to power steering being outside the customer's price range, a more likely strategy will be to emphasise other aspects of the car included in the price. One can begin to see that the success of the salesperson is likely to rest with his or her ability to identify accurately the causes of customer behaviour.

Interpersonal attributions are also important in the workplace, because the way in which we explain another person's behaviour can influence both how we feel about that person and how we behave towards him or her. Common situations which trigger interpersonal attributions include surprising and unusual or un-pleasant behaviour by colleagues, clients or supervisors. If any-one requires further persuasion as to the prevalence of interpersonal attributions in the workplace, one only has to point to the popularity of gossip. People often enjoy gossiping, an ac-tivity that permeates most, if not all, organisations!

One form of interpersonal attribution that has been of particu-lar interest to occupational psychologists is that of supervisor attributions for employee behaviour. As an example let's take John, a supervisor in a packaging warehouse, responsible for 20 employees. One of the employees for whom he is responsible, Monica, has worked in the section for about three months. Her early performance was excellent. She was cheerful, always punctual and ready to learn new tasks. Recently, however, her behaviour has changed. She is often late and her performance has deteriorated to the extent that she is barely doing the minimum required of her. It is unlikely that many supervisors will react immediately with penalties; instead they will try to understand *why* Monica's performance has deteriorated. Here John's task is to identify the possible causes of this deterioration and decide which of these is the most likely explanation. One possibility may be that Monica is experiencing difficulties at home; John knows that her husband has become ill and has had to take time off work. Another possibility is that Monica has moved to another work group that contains several people that John describes as 'troublemakers'. Monica may be finding it difficult to fit in. Alternatively, it is always possible that Monica's early behaviour was simply a honeymoon period and her 'true colours' are beginning to emerge. Perhaps she really does have less motivation and enthusiasm than John at first imagined. Finally, John could attribute Monica's behaviour to his own supervisory style and the more relaxed attitude he has begun to take towards her.

Clearly, the way in which John explains Monica's behaviour will influence his decision whether he should: (a) use punitive powers; (b) engage in a private discussion with Monica; (c) provide assistance such as compassionate leave; (d) tackle the group troublemakers; (e) move Monica to a different group; (f) provide additional training; (g) change his own management style; or (h) use a combination of the above. The causal attribution that he makes and his subsequent behaviour will also have an effect upon the ongoing working relationship between him and Monica. A misattribution could, potentially, lead to a disenchanted employee, reduce motivation still further and increase levels of animosity in the workplace.

It is probably not surprising, given the important implications that supervisors' attributions can have for successful work relations, that a large amount of research has focused on improving their accuracy. By doing so, it has been claimed that supervisors will become more fair and effective managers of people and better able to facilitate high levels of performance from their teams. One approach has been to alert supervisors to what has been described as 'the fundamental attributional error', a bias to which we are all vulnerable. It is a tendency for people to over-emphasise the importance of dispositional causes (such as lack of motivation, poor skills) when explaining others' behaviour, and underestimate the role of situational causes (such as inade-quate training, organisational expectations). For supervisor at-tributions, however, the implications for situations such as appraisal interviews are extensive.

Another common attributional bias of which supervisors need to be aware is the 'self-serving bias'. This is another common tendency to attribute positive outcomes to internal causes and negative outcomes to external causes. Two common explana-tions for why this bias occurs have been posited. The first sug-gests that by externalising the causes of failure and bad events while internalising the causes of positive events, we can main-tain positive self-esteem. Consequently, the bias serves a protec-tive function. The second interpretation is that the bias fulfils a self-presentational function. By internalising positive and exter-nalising negative events, people can convey a more favourable impression of themselves. With supervisors, attributions for em-ployee behaviour can also have personal relevance and may be subject to the self-serving attributional bias. For example, poor employee performance attributed to lack of ability on the part of the employee is a lot less threatening to a manager than attribut-ing it to poor supervisory style or a failure to identify training needs. Of course, the down side to a manager externalising blame is that he or she may be perceived by superiors as evad-ing responsibility. Evidence suggests that supervisors who are least confident in their own abilities are the ones most likely to internalise credit and externalise blame!

Intergroup attributions

Intergroup attributions are causal explanations that members of one group make for either outcomes involving their own group or outcomes involving members of another group. They can result from perceived as well as actual membership of particular groups. In the workplace, for example, employees who work in manufacturing may consider themselves a quite separate and distinct group from their colleagues in marketing and sales, even if they work for the same organisation. Similarly, different cells on a manufacturing production line are often treated as independent groups or teams by organisations to facilitate a degree of competitiveness and enhance performance.

Common biases in intergroup attributions such as the 'ultimate attributional bias' act to increase this competition. This bias is a tendency for members of one group to enhance the positive outcomes and minimise the negative outcomes associated with members of their own 'in-group'. For example, members of a marketing team might attribute the success of an advertising campaign in which they have been involved to their team's expertise at identifying innovative ways of selling products—internal, stable and controllable causes. On the other hand, a product 'flop' is more likely to be dismissed in terms of unstable or uncontrollable causes, such as the introduction of a similar, but cheaper, product by a competitor. When explaining outcomes associated with 'out-groups', however, attributions tend to minimise positive outcomes such as good performance and emphasise negative outcomes such as failure. Consequently, a successful advertising campaign put together by a competitor's marketing team might be attributed to luck rather than skill, and any failure to a lack of expertise rather than more situational causes. While the ultimate attributional error can prove useful in enhancing competition between groups, it can result in disharmony and increased workplace conflict unless managed appropriately.

As mentioned earlier, intergroup attributions can result from perceived and actual group membership. This can become problematic in the workplace when an employee's membership of a group not defined by work (such as gender or race) is perceived by others to be stronger than their membership of the work group. For example, a black candidate may be associated with 'out-group' status (although often unconsciously) by a white interviewer. If the interviewer's attributions for the black candidate's behaviour are then vulnerable to the ultimate attributional bias, the result would be an emphasis upon negative outcomes and less emphasis on positive outcomes. Thus, intergroup attributions may contribute to unfair discrimination in selection interviews. Similarly, considerable evidence suggests that very different attributions are made for male and female employee behaviour. Overall, good job performance is more often described as 'luck' for a woman, but is generally seen as 'skill' for a man. This is particularly so when the job is perceived as typically 'masculine'—a situation that is, unfortunately, still predominantly the case when we consider management positions.

Comparatively little research has been done to investigate intergroup attributions in the workplace. However, one might argue that increasing globalisation of organisations, with the associated need for employees to work alongside colleagues from different countries and cultures, will see an increase in the importance of intergroup attributions. We already know that certain attributional patterns are not universal. For example, employees in Western organisations are more likely to describe their successes in terms of ego-enhancing attributions (*I was successful because of the effort I made*). Conversely, employees in Eastern organisations more typically display 'modesty biases' or attributions that emphasise the importance of the contributions of others (*I was successful because of the support of the team*). Therefore, cultural differences in the way employees from different countries behave, and intergroup biases, could have important implications for the successful functioning of multinational teams.

Organisational attributions

The fourth level of attributions—organisational attributions— refers to causal attributions for events or behaviours shared by individuals within organisations. Causal attributions are most often described in terms of phenomena which occur as a consequence of a person witnessing an event directly. However, attributions can also be learned second hand from other people. Quite simply, it is not possible for people to witness all the events that could be important to them. Consequently, explanations produced by other people and shared through communication are also likely to be adopted and, as such, serve as a secondary source of causal knowledge.

Similarly in an organisation, employees will depend upon causal attributions learned from other people, including managers and colleagues. This sharing of causal attributions between members of an organisation is particularly important in the socialisation of new employees or team members. For example, Tom has recently moved from the accounting department to sales, and joined a new work team. As part of his socialisation into the team, other members will explain to him why he is expected to behave in a particular way. For example, 'newcomers always make the tea'; 'Martin is allowed to get away with being late in the morning (he is in with the boss)'; 'he should always try to keep on the right side of Maureen (because the boss's secretary can make or break your career in this section)'. In addition, it will be the responsibility of his manager to explain why he is expected to behave in a particular way and, by doing so, to pass on those shared attributions condoned by the organisation.

Senior organisational personnel engage in sense-making at a strategic level. The result of this 'sense-making' is corporate level causal attributions that are subsequently communicated to employees within the company. They might include the following attributions, for instance: 'we are restructuring this section to make the business more cost-effective' or 'we expect individuals to answer telephone calls by the second ring because this presents a positive image of the company to our customers'. Organisational attributions can be communicated by word of mouth during meetings, via company literature such as company reports, or through training programmes. However, causal attributions produced by senior personnel as explanations for why the organisation is doing well or badly, are likely to influence the organisation as a whole. For example, a sudden decline in profitability on a particular line must be accounted for. It could be a design failure: the product does not do what it is supposed to do. Alternatively, poor sales figures could reflect poor performance by the sales function, one solution to which could be restructuring and further training. The decline might be attributed to the introduction of a similar but a cheaper product by a competitor—in which case senior managers may move to invest in additional marketing and advertising. In contrast, the same sales downturn attributed to a growing need for additional and more modern manufacturing equipment, is likely to result in funds being directed away from other business areas into purchase of equipment. Clearly, at this strategic level organisational attributions have a much wider impact upon organisational functioning.

Although attributions are used to change behaviour and attitudes of individuals within the organisation, they can also play an important role in changing attitudes and behaviour of those external to the organisation such as shareholders, clients, competitors and customers. Organisational attributions play a part in attempts at strategic impression management. For example, they feature prominently in company annual reports where the letter to shareholders from the chief executive officer is normally replete with causal attributions. These include explanations for why the company has failed to meet prior objectives, for example, an unforeseen and sudden downturn in the economy. They may also include explanations for exceeding targets set at the beginning of the year, for example, the company was very effective at identifying new markets and adapting its structure to cope with a changing environment. As the LACS permits the analysis of causal attributions in written and spoken form, analysing these attributions in detail is quite possible. One possibility worth exploring would be the extent to which patterns of organisational attributions produced over a sequence of annual reports were associated with organisational performance, measured by external criteria such as value of shares on the stock market.

Finally, the use of organisational attributions in strategic impression management extends to the excuses and causal accounts offered by companies for a failure in service or a defective product. One example of this was provided by a colleague who had returned a defective food item to the manufacturer. In the letter of apology she received from the company they apologised for the condition of the item, but by way of explanation stated that they had been experiencing difficulties with employees on that particular food line—an interesting case of externalising blame to the actions taken by employees for whom the organisation is ultimately responsible. In the UK, the now defunct British Rail has been responsible for some amusing causal attributions explaining delays in service. These have included trains slowed by 'the wrong type of snow' and 'leaves on the tracks'. Such causes would be coded as external and uncontrollable using the LACS. They are defensive attributions designed to convey the impression that it was not the fault of British Rail. However, attributions do not make effective excuses if the customer believes that the company is simply trying to evade responsibility. A new opportunity for attributions explaining delays in rail journeys in the UK has been provided by the recent separation of Railtrack, responsible for the rail infrastructure, and the companies running passenger services. The latter, who have almost exclusive access to passengers sitting on delayed trains, now have the opportunity to externalise responsibility to another company for the condition of tracks, signals or any other problems on the line.

ATTRIBUTIONAL CODING AND WORKPLACE ATTRIBUTIONS: CASE EXAMPLES

Having shown the prevalence and importance of workplace attributions, valuable information concerning individual, group and organisational behaviour could clearly be gained by investigating them further. Traditional organisational research has been dominated by a reliance upon quantitative methods such as the questionnaire or strictly qualitative methods such as the interview. However, attributional coding using the LACS can be seen as a bridge between a quantitative and qualitative approach. It can be used to explore in a quantitative way the patterns of attributions generated by organisational members through discourse. This discourse might occur in several settings: semi-structured interviews, unstructured team meetings, negotiations between management and unions, discussions between salespeople and their clients, appraisal and selection interviews, and attributions written in company documents such as reports, training materials, letters to stakeholders and company mission statements. By using the specified coding system in the LACS to code what can often be many hundreds of attributional statements, generating very rich data is possible. The statistical analysis of these data enables both the analyses of unique idiographic patterns of attributions produced by individual employees and the nomothetic patterns of attributions held by members of particular groups. Thus, comparing the attributions produced by different groups and tracking any change in attributions over time is possible. For example, manufacturing groups might be compared with sales and marketing, or engineers from the same company but working in different countries.

The following three examples have been chosen to illustrate how the LACS can be used to explore three different types of workplace attributions. The first of these examples looks at intrapersonal attributions made by candidates during selection interviews. Although examples of attributions produced during selection interviews were presented in Chapter 2, this example will describe the research in more detail. The study set out to investigate the relationship between interviewers' decisions regarding the selection of a particular candidate and the candidate's attributions for previous behaviour and outcomes. The second example describes a project carried out with a national retail organisation which explored causal attributions produced by sales staff for successful and unsuccessful customer interactions. This example focuses on intrapersonal and interpersonal attributions. Finally, the third example illustrates how attributional coding can be used to explore organisational attributions. It describes a project that investigated potential cross-cultural differences in attributions produced by German and UK engineers within a multinational organisation for a recent culture-change programme.

Attributional coding and the selection interview

The selection interview has many critics. It has been damned as subjective, unreliable and vulnerable to bias, but according to recent surveys it remains the most popular method for recruiting new employees. As the selection interview is unlikely to go away, spending more time understanding how selection decisions are made, and identifying potential means for improving its predictive validity, seems reasonable.

Several different researchers have proposed that causal attributions play a central role in the selection interview. Both interviewer and interviewees are trying to make sense of one another and, based upon the information they gain, to take a decision about whether to continue the employment relationship. It is the interviewer's task to find out more about the candidate, to explore previous behaviour and predict how the candidate is likely to behave in future work situations. The interviewer is keen to know why the candidate has acted in specific ways: why she took one summer job rather than another; why she is applying for this job; why she changed courses in the second year at university. Peter Herriot has argued that these causal attributions will directly influence selection decisions. For example, faced with a candidate who switched degree courses in her second year, an interviewer may attribute the change to 'initiative', an internal, controllable and relatively positive cause. Alternatively he or she may attribute the change of course to the candidate's inability to cope, a much less favourable attribution.

Although interviewers may formulate their own causal attributions for candidate behaviour (and having read the application form may have done so even before the interview started), an important second source of attributions in the selection interview are the candidates themselves. Candidates are asked for causal attributions directly, as in 'Why did you apply to study French?'. They also enter the selection interview with the expectation that they must justify their suitability for that particular job. As illustrated in Chapter 2, the selection interview is an ideal scenario for analysing public or spoken attributions. The following excerpt was taken from a graduate recruitment interview. The candidate is applying to do her articles (the second stage of qualifying as a solicitor in the UK) with a firm of solicitors in the City of London.

INTERVIEWER: *So why have you applied to city firms? Have you applied to mainly large firms?*

CANDIDATE: *Yes, I think it's because . . . I think it's the attraction of London. I mean, you know, it's the heart of commerce and I think that's the direction I'd like to go in with my work. As I said earlier, you know, the range of activities that go on there, it would be a very good experience for me and hopefully I'll find something that I really want to end up doing 'cos I'm not definite about the exact area I want and hopefully I'll find that.*
INTERVIEWER: *What attributes do you think you've got that will lend you to life in the City?*
CANDIDATE: *Well I think I'd be quite good with clients because I find it very easy to talk to people. I've met loads of people with my hobbies and I get used to having to work with teams with things like orchestras and groups, you know.*

This extract clearly illustrates the richness of attributional statements elicited from selection interview transcripts. Not only does the interviewer directly request attributions *'why have you applied to city firms?'*, the candidate also spontaneously produces a string of causes: *'it's . . . the attraction of London', 'it's the heart of commerce and that's the direction I'd like to go in', 'the range of activities', 'it would be a good experience for me'* and *'hopefully I'll find something I really want to do'*. In response to this one question the interviewer is already presented with a series of causal attributions. Typically a 30-minute graduate recruitment interview (which includes 20 minutes of questioning by the interviewer and a further 10 minutes of questions from the candidate) can generate between 40 and 80 attributions spoken by candidates. An important task of the interviewer is to sort through the attributions produced by candidates and, ideally, identify patterns in the way they have explained their actions.

The study described here in brief refers to research carried out investigating spoken attributions and candidate success in graduate recruitment interviews (see Silvester, 1997). The main aim was to discover whether candidates who are rated as more suitable for selection by interviewers produce different attributions to those of unsuccessful candidates. It was based upon the premise that spoken attributions act as clues for interviewers who are looking to predict the candidate's likely level of motivation in future work situations. Surprisingly, virtually no research has explored what candidates actually *say* in selection interviews, let alone the types of attributions that they produce. The broad hypotheses of the study were that successful candidates would produce more internal and controllable attributions for events than unsuccessful candidates.

Two companies took part in the study: a national distribution company and a large firm of solicitors in the City of London. The research involved tape-recording graduate recruitment interviews and naturally required the permission of both interviewers and candidates. It also entailed collection of report forms completed by interviewers following each interview that rated the candidate on several job-related criteria such as 'leadership potential', 'motivation' and 'communication skills'. After all attributional coding had been completed, the overall rating for each candidate was compared with the pattern of attributions each had produced. This was done to ensure that the researcher did not have any knowledge of the candidate's rating prior to the extraction and coding of attributions that could, potentially, have influenced the process.

We tape-recorded a total of 35 selection interviews. These were then transcribed verbatim and all individual attributional statements extracted. In this study we identified 1,967 attributional statements. Each of these statements was then coded on five causal dimensions. This made it possible to build up a substantial quantitative database, permitting us to compare patterns of attributions produced by successful candidates and unsuccessful candidates. It is worth noting at this point that all of the standard LACS coding definitions, except 'Global', were used to code statements in this study. The global dimension is the most subject to contextual differences, and experience suggests that the researcher may need to define this dimension further to suit the situation for which it is being used. In this selection interview research we defined 'global' in terms of whether or not a cause could be considered to have an influence on career outcomes (e.g. choice of degree, summer placement with an organisation).

Overall, approximately twice as many extracted attributions related to positive outcomes than negative outcomes. Positive attributions usually referred to incidents such as a candidate describing the causes of his or her success on a particular task (*'I got the summer job because of my experience the previous year'*).

Negative attributions were more likely to concern excuses for previous failures or justifications for outcomes that had not worked out as expected. The attributional patterns produced by groups of successful and unsuccessful candidates for positive and negative outcomes were explored separately. Interestingly, while no differences were found between successful and unsuccessful candidates in their attributions for positive outcomes, differences were found for negative outcomes.

Figure 4.1 illustrates a comparison of the proportions of negative attributions made by successful and unsuccessful candidates during selection interviews with the distribution company. Overall, when candidates were asked about previous failures, those who were rated more favourably tended to make attributions that involved more stable, global, internal, personal and controllable causes. The fact that they attribute negative outcomes to more internal and controllable causes, fits with Weiner's (1986) suggestion. Individuals who see the causes of failure as things that they can learn to control and therefore avoid in future are more likely to change their behaviour.

Besides investigating candidate attributions, follow-up interviews with interviewers were carried out in an attempt to identify what interviewers considered the 'ideal' candidate. One interviewer, a partner in the law firm, made the following comment:

I got criticised for turning one candidate down who had absolutely outstanding qualifications. I mean they were absolutely extra-

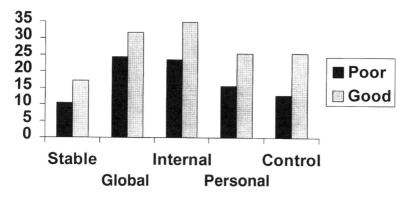

Figure 4.1 Proportions of negative attributions produced by candidates in selection interview

ordinarily good qualifications, obviously going for a first class degree,
had all A's at A level, all B's at O Level. Except for one which was
grade C in English Language. And almost as an ice-breaking question
I asked how that had come about and got the answer . . . not God
alone knows, I must have had a bad day or something like that. It was
oh well obviously the examiners can't have marked that paper cor-
rectly, because I certainly didn't do any worse in that paper than any
of the others and I'm quite confident in my own mind that I got a
grade A. I put in a grade A standard performance.

Now if that's the sort of attitude that someone has—I mean it
would be disastrous in practice, because even if you don't ever make a
mistake with a client, a client is always going to eventually think that
you have. You will always write something, a piece of advice, which
isn't exactly what they wanted when they asked you. And it is a
disaster to blame the client, to say 'well it's your fault you didn't tell
me to do that'. It's much better to say 'oh I'm terribly sorry Fred, I'll
write to you, I'll correct that and send you a revised letter tomorrow'.

This extract is a good illustration of how a candidate's attributions
serve an important impression management function during the
selection interview. By externalising responsibility for his C grade
and blaming the examiner for poor marking, the candidate fails to
convey the impression that he has learned from his experience. In
addition, the interviewer, rightly or wrongly, assumes that he
might respond similarly towards clients in future. There is unlikely to be a direct relationship between candidate attributions
and interviewer selection decisions. Other factors, including candidate experience and skills and interviewer bias, are likely to
play a part. However, the results of the study do suggest that the
way in which candidates explain themselves in interviews serves
to moderate interviewer decisions. Further research would certainly be worth while. Other interesting areas where a similar
approach might be taken include appraisal situations and the way
in which defendants present themselves in trials.

Attributions for sales outcomes

In an earlier section we argued that causal attributions are inte-
gral to sales situations. We suggested that attributions made by

a salesperson for a customer's behaviour *during* an interaction can guide the salesperson's decision about which strategy to adopt and how to adapt one's behaviour to meet a customer's needs best. We also proposed that the type of attributions that salespeople make *following* successful and unsuccessful sales interactions influence how they respond in similar future situations. Research evidence seems to support these claims. For example, Martin Seligman found that insurance salespeople who possessed more optimistic attributional styles sold more insurance than those with a pessimistic attributional style. However, Seligman used the Attributional Style Questionnaire (ASQ), asking respondents to nominate and rate causes of hypothetical outcomes. The outcomes they rated were unrelated to the sales situation (e.g. 'you receive a promotion at work' or 'you do not get the job that you applied for'). He did not look at attributions for actual sales situations, including interactions with customers. We know surprisingly little about attributions of this type.

The following example illustrates how the LACS was used to identify and extract (but not code) causal attributions, produced by sales assistants in a large national UK retail organisation, for actual sales situations. The project was designed as a qualitative exploration of whether 'good' and 'poor' retail staff (as rated by their managers) make different attributions for successful and unsuccessful sales interactions. It was part of a larger investigation to develop a questionnaire for selecting sales assistants (see Patterson & Silvester, 1998).

In any retail organisation the performance of sales assistants is crucial for ensuring high levels of sales, good relationships with customers and continuing customer loyalty. The role of the sales assistant in the company involved in this study is typical of that found in many other retail environments. Sales assistants are expected to be proactive in approaching customers and creating sales. They are also required to help customers by providing product information or showing them where to find a product. Sales assistants are expected to work on the till and ensure that shelves and products are well presented. In a recent evaluation of the sales assistant role, this company had identified what they described as two essential criteria for successful job performance:

'customer care' and 'sales performance'. These were described as distinct criteria that, in combination, would ensure high levels of sales achieved *through* excellent customer care.

Although one might argue that sales overall do not occur without customer care, a case can be made for sales performance and customer care being quite different aspects of a sales assistant's behaviour. Certain companies train their salespeople to attain high sales without a strong emphasis on customer care. Here the role is seen more as manipulating a customer into a sale using particular sales strategies. In this situation a sales assistant's pay is likely to depend, at least in part, upon the amount that he or she sells. An example of this would be telephone sales using cold-calling. Here the primary motivator is achieving a sale; building a long-term relationship with the customer comes a poor second. Insurance selling can often exemplify this approach. However, sales performance prioritised over customer care could be viewed as a successful strategy when the likelihood of an ongoing relationship with a customer is low (e.g. they are making an expensive 'one-off' purchase). For most retail organisations, however, the creation and maintenance of long-term customer relationships are essential. Sales are not viewed simply as the product of customer manipulation. The responsibility of the sales assistant is to foster a positive relationship based upon good customer care. One purpose of the following study was to explore whether findings from attribution research investigating close personal relationships might help explain the way in which sales assistants attempt to foster positive relationships with customers.

A total of 30 male and female sales assistants from stores across the UK took part in individual semi-structured critical incident interviews. The sales assistants were told that the interviews were being carried out to understand more about the causes of successful and unsuccessful situations at work. They were also assured that their responses would be anonymous. The interviews included questions that asked the sales assistants to think of situations, in which they or their colleagues had been involved, that had gone either particularly well or particularly badly. All interviews were audiotaped and then transcribed with causal attributions subsequently extracted.

Attributions for sales performance

It was anticipated that sales assistants who were rated as 'good' by their managers would be more likely to believe that they could exert an influence over a sales outcome; that is, they would be more likely to attribute a sale to something that they did (e.g. approach and persuade the customer) rather than to an external cause (e.g. a customer's need, or low price). This hypothesis was borne out in conversations with managers who could all provide examples of poor sales assistants whom, despite training, continued to believe that customers generally only bought a product because they needed it. Although all staff had received training in how to approach customers and influence a sale, poor sales staff did not seem to consider themselves an agent of the sale. For example, one sales assistant rated as 'poor' by her manager made the following comments:

> *Sometimes sales really go well—it depends what type of customer it is. But there was one customer who just approached me. I wasn't really talking I was just being normal. She was the one who was being friendly to me, so I was really friendly back to her. Yeh, she started the conversation up and it was an interesting one, so we were like talking and we were both happy.*

Here the salesperson attributes success at selling to 'the type of customer'—a common response from poor sales assistants interviewed. Several commented that 'sometimes you see people selling something to a customer and you know that they're that type of customer—you know—someone you can sell anything to'. Here the cause of a successful sale is seen as external and uncontrollable, something that they cannot be expected to influence greatly. In the excerpt above, the sales assistant makes several external attributions where she describes the customer as an agent and herself as a target: 'she was the one who was being friendly to me, so I was really friendly back to her' and 'she started the conversation up . . . , so we were like talking and we were both happy'. There is no evidence of the sales assistant taking a proactive or influential role.

In contrast the interviews provided evidence that successful sales assistants believed that they could influence the sale, perhaps by persuading the customer to buy another product as well. The following example is of a male employee describing his involvement in what he sees as a good sales outcome:

> *When I came here I was given tights to look after. I mean it sounded absolutely ridiculous at first. One of my colleagues suggested I should model the tights myself. I had to take the video home to watch, read up some books and get to know about lycra and things like that. And then when customers came in with problems—they would want this colour or that, I was able to help them. It made me feel like I could adjust to any situation. One customer came in and she wanted me to suggest a colour. I looked through the section and I was able to suggest one even though I don't wear tights. I just managed to remember her face and then next time she was in I asked her if she liked the tights and she said yes—they were the ones that she was wearing. So now everytime she has a problem she comes back to me.*

Imagining a more difficult scenario than a man being expected to sell an essentially female product to a woman customer is hard. It is a situation where externalising the causes of any failure would be quite easy for the sales assistant: 'women don't like to take advice from men about which tights they should wear' or 'women are usually too embarrassed to ask a man questions about stockings'. Nevertheless, in this example, although the male sales assistant describes the origin of the sale in terms of the customer approaching him, he continues by making internal attributions. He could give her information and he possessed sufficient knowledge to help the customer because he had taken the video home and read the books about lycra. The sales assistant also makes an internal attribution for the subsequent sales outcome—he could remember the customer's name and approach her, so now if she has a problem she always returns to him for advice. This sales assistant believes that he can influence outcomes and the confidence he has gained through learning about the product and being able to advise the customer has enabled him to approach other customers. Besides attributions for their own success or failure in sales situations, sales assistants can often recognise why a colleague is so successful and will make internal attributions for their success with a customer:

I remember this customer that came in and wanted some things for his holiday. It was my colleague who dealt with him. The customer had only come in for about two items, but she ended up by selling him a bag of holiday stuff. She got the leaflet out for him and suggested this and suggested that. She explained why he might need different things and in the end I think he bought about £98 worth of stuff. I was really impressed.

Attributions for customer care

The second criterion 'customer care' can also be defined in attributional terms. While 'sales performance' can be explained in terms of research concerned with attributions and motivation to achieve, 'customer care' relates more to research concerned with attributions and close personal relationships. For the latter, attributions have been found to moderate the quality of interpersonal relationships. The way in which, for example, a man explains his partner's behaviour influences how he feels about that behaviour, how he responds, and the success of the ongoing relationship. These findings have relevance for how sales assistants explain customer behaviour. The following excerpt describes a situation of good customer care:

I had a gentleman the other day who wanted a box of chocolates. I was actually on cash and wrap at the time, but I took him to the section where the chocolates were. And then he wanted some little glass bowls so I told him that they were down the aisle and on the right. He was happy so I left him there and went back to cash and wrap. But it was quite quiet at the time so I went along to make sure he had found the right place and he was very happy because I had gone out of my way to serve him. And I said you can pay at my till if you like and he was really thankful and pleased.

In this case the sales assistant attributes the successful customer interaction to internal and controllable causes such as making sure the customer found the product and offering further help. She describes herself as proactive in much the same way as a good sales assistant describing a successful sale. She could influence the outcome. However, attributions also play an important part in difficult customer interactions and it is the way in which sales assistants explain conflict that can provide an insight into their ability to generate long-term positive customer interactions. Take the following example from a good salesperson:

I mean we get customers who come in with faulty goods and provided you handle them properly and you agree with them 'yes it's definitely faulty' and it really shouldn't have gone wrong after so long, then they are not difficult. I don't think I've had any bad experiences with faulty goods because you've just got to talk to customers. If a customer comes in in an angry mood you've just got to try to diffuse the situation. I think it's 'cos of the way you handle the customer. I mean the last thing that they want you to say is 'oh no you can't have a refund' or 'no it's not faulty'. If you agree with them they are quite happy and then you turn it back and say 'what would you like me to do?'. Because people with faulty goods come in quite angry especially if it's something that they've only had for a month or two, they're ready for a fight. So you've got to turn it around and calm it down so there's not a fight.

Conflict is inevitable in retail situations. A customer may complain about a product, or the service they had received or they may be in a hurry when several other customers are waiting. Often the customer may be quite justified in complaining, but it is the way in which the sales assistant deals with this situation that determines whether the conflict is exacerbated or resolved. Most companies train their sales staff in how to deal with these situations. Employees are encouraged to 'own the problem', listen to the customer, apologise and accept responsibility on behalf of the company while not taking matters personally. However, certain individuals are more threatened by conflict situations than others. These employees find it more difficult to 'own the problem' and when faced with a complaint are more likely to externalise the cause. While such a strategy may help the individual to protect self-esteem, it can exacerbate conflict, particularly when a sales assistant externalises and blames the customer. Take the following excerpt from an interview with an employee rated as 'poor' by her manager. As part of the interview she is asked to think of a situation with a customer that did not go particularly well and what she thought might have caused it:

There was one time when I was working on the till and a man wanted to pay for a chocolate bar. He pulled a whole handful of coins out of his pocket and out of all the coins he had he chose a really horrible coin and gave it to me. And I thought 'out of all those coins why did he have to give me this one?' And so I said to him 'I'm not going to accept this', because it was really horrible, you couldn't even see the Queen's head on it. And then he goes 'why won't you accept it?' and I said—well I can't remember what I said, but we were arguing. I don't know, maybe I was in a bad mood. But I really think he deliberately gave me that coin, and I really felt I shouldn't take it. But my friend next to me whispered 'just take it' so I took it. I didn't want to argue any more over one little coin.

In this example, the employee admits that she may have been in a bad mood that day. However, she clearly thinks the argument was caused by the customer deliberately choosing an old and dirty coin with which to pay. She has externalised the cause and attributed it to an internal and controllable cause on the part of the customer. This pattern of attributing bears strong similarities to that displayed by partners in distressed close relationships, where individuals are more likely to blame their partners for negative outcomes. In contrast, individuals in successful personal relationships are more likely to give credit to their partner for positive outcomes and accept more responsibility themselves for negative outcomes.

Clearly, a more detailed exploration using the LACS of the attributions produced by sales assistants has provided considerable insight into the way in which these attributions moderate customer interactions and sales outcomes. Following on from this research we have been able to use these extracted attributions to design a selection questionnaire which is now being used throughout the company, alongside other selection tools, to select retail sales assistants.

Organisational attributions

The final case study describes how the LACS has been used to explore organisational attributions made by German and UK engineers for the causes of perceived success or failure of a culture-change programme. For more detail see Silvester, Ferguson and

Patterson (1997). The study had two broad aims. The first was to identify whether or not the LACS could prove a useful method for investigating shared organisational attributions. The second was to explore possible cultural differences in attributions produced by engineers in the UK and Germany who work for the same multinational organisation.

One important reason for exploring organisational attributions is their likely relationship with organisational culture. The idea of organisational culture has generated a tremendous amount of interest in recent years. Many companies have invested heavily in attempts to identify what particular type of culture they possess, and also efforts to change their present culture into a new strong and unified one. The motive behind such investment rests with the claim that organisations that possess strong and uniform cultures are likely to demonstrate higher levels of performance. Unfortunately few methods are available for analysing or quantifying organisational culture, and researchers have found it difficult to define what is meant by the term 'organisational culture'. The various definitions that exist include 'a system of publicly and collectively accepted meanings that operate for a group at a particular time' (Trice & Beyer, 1984); a pattern of 'basic assumptions' developed as the group or organisation learns to cope with its environment (Schein, 1985), and, more simply, 'the way we do things around here' (Deal & Kennedy, 1982).

In previous work conducted with this organisation we defined organisational culture in terms of the causal attributions shared by individual employees for organisational events (Silvester, Anderson & Patterson, in press). Through the communication of causal attributions, individuals within organisations come to share common explanations for events. By doing so they are better able to negotiate their environment and act in a way that is consistent with their colleagues within the organisation. Consequently, rather than describing organisational culture as 'the way we do things around here', an attributional interpretation would describe it in terms of 'why we do things in that way around here'. It was proposed that causal attributions could be viewed as 'cognitive building blocks' of organisational culture. Furthermore, one way of assessing the 'strength' of an organisation's culture might simply be to assess the extent to which individuals share the same causal attributions for particular organisational events.

The company involved in the study was a multinational manufacturing organisation that had recently introduced a large-scale culture-change programme based upon the principles of Total Quality Management (TQM). The programme initially involved training engineers in the UK and Germany in the principles of TQM. A central aim of this training was to give engineers the interpersonal skills deemed necessary for effective cross-functional team working. It was anticipated that a culture change would be effected throughout the company by changing the way in which engineers behaved. Engineers were given 37 days off-the-job training grouped into seven modules and, at the time of the project, this training was being provided to more than 4,000 engineers in the UK and Germany.

The company was initially interested in using the LACS as a method for exploring the beliefs held by employees about the causes of, or potential barriers to, success of the culture-change programme. An initial study compared attributions produced by trainers, trainees and managers in the UK (Silvester, Anderson & Patterson, in press). We found substantial differences in the way each of these three groups construed the success (or otherwise) of the culture-change programme. The study described here followed on from the earlier investigation. It was prompted by the desire to explore potential differences in the way in which engineers taking part in the programme in Germany and the UK construed the potential success of the culture-change programme differently.

Although little research has compared attributions produced by individuals in different cultures, evidence suggests that the attributional patterns found in Western populations are not universal. For example, it has been found that Taiwanese employees typically adopt a 'modesty bias' when describing the causes of their own successful work performance. They are more likely to attribute their success at work to external causes such as the contribution of other team members or their managers. In contrast, employees in the West displayed a self-serving bias where success is more likely to be attributed to internal and controllable causes such as increased effort or ability.

Six UK and five German engineers were interviewed in English using a semi-structured interview format. Topics included questions about the success of the programme, potential barriers to the programme, what they expected it to achieve, and how they thought it might influence organisational culture. All of the participants were chosen at random from the engineers who had participated in the study. They were interviewed in English, because this was the operating language of the organisation and all employees were expected to be able to converse comfortably with colleagues in this language. All interviews lasted about an hour and were audiotaped. They were later transcribed and attributions extracted for attributional coding. These attributions were coded using a modified version of the LACS with fewer attributional dimensions.

Agent–target

Because the primary focus was on attributions concerning the success or otherwise of the culture-change programme, the Agent and Target codings were restricted to 'Company', 'Change Programme'. An example of an attribution where the Agent was coded as Company and the Target as Change Programme would be: *'The change programme is likely to be successful if the company makes sure that there is enough time for engineers to attend.'* Similarly, an attribution in which the Agent is Change Programme and the Target Company would be: *'Provided enough engineers are trained there should be a sea-change in attitudes across the company.'*

Positive–negative

Causal attributions were also coded according to whether they referred to a Negative outcome (e.g. *'There's not much chance of my attending a course given that our section is so short staffed'*) or a Positive or neutral outcome (e.g. *'Since our team leader went on the course our meetings are always much better organised'*).

Stable–unstable

We have already mentioned that when using the LACS the researcher may need to define the causal dimensions to meet the needs of the context further in which the research is taking place. However, in terms of this study, Stable was defined according to the definition as provided in the LACS. A cause was coded Stable if it could be considered to have an ongoing and relatively permanent effect upon outcomes within the organisation. So, for example, an attribution coded Stable would be: *'The change programme is likely to continue because the company is committed to long-term change.'* An example of an attribution coded Unstable would be: *'Everyone is so positive on the course, but once you get back to where you work it's so hard to put everything into practice.'*

Global–specific

This dimension refers to how widespread or important the consequences of the cause are perceived to be. For the purposes of this study a Global cause was defined as one which could be expected to influence relatively important outcomes throughout the company. A Specific cause was defined as one that has a more limited influence upon a specific individual or group. So, for example, a Global attribution would be *'After all these changes people can see a future, they're beginning to feel better about the company'* and a Specific attribution, *'Going on the programme has meant that I begin my meetings with a warm-up session'*.

Actual–hypothetical

Besides the usual LACS coding categories, a further category was included. We were specifically interested in whether the attributions that engineers produced referred to 'Actual' outcomes, or 'Hypothetical' outcomes that may or may not occur in future. Little attention has been paid to the distinction between attributions for actual events and attributions for events that, in the opinion of the person being interviewed, might occur in future provided certain conditions are fulfilled. This distinction was of particular interest in the case of attributions for the culture-change programme. It was anticipated as a method of distinguishing between the extent to which employees believed that change had actually occurred following the culture-change programme and that change might occur in future. For example, *'I've noticed that those people who have been on the programme are starting to change their behaviour during team meetings'* would be coded Actual as the attribution refers to the cause of an actual change in behaviour. However, *'I think the programme will be successful provided there is more support from management'* would be coded Hypothetical. Although it refers to a positive outcome (the programme being successful), the outcome is hypothetical in that it requires certain conditions (support from management) to occur.

Results

In total, 419 causal attributions were extracted from the 11 interviews: 160 attributions from the five interviews with German engineers and 259 from the six interviews with UK engineers. A comparison of attributions made by German and UK engineers revealed that engineers in the UK made proportionately more negative attributions (59.1%) than German engineers (30%). Proportions of attributions are used rather than actual numbers of attributions because it overcomes potential problems associated with the different numbers of attributions produced by each group. This suggests that German engineers talked more positively about outcomes in general during the interviews. However, because attributions are coded for different agents and on different causal dimensions, we could explore the differences between types of attributions in much more detail.

For example, the first comparison, based simply upon Actual versus Hypothetical codings compared attributions made by German and UK engineers where the Agent had been identified as the Change Programme (Table 4.1).

It is clear from Table 4.1 that German and UK engineers make similar numbers of positive attributions for the Change Programme, but that the distribution of whether they refer to Actual

TABLE 4.1 Attributions for change programme as agent of positive outcomes by country

	UK engineers		German engineers	
Attributions for Actual events	26	(56.5%)	31	(70.5%)
Attributions for Hypothetical events	20	(43.5%)	13	(29.5%)
Total	46		44	

or Hypothetical outcomes is quite different. The German engineers make proportionately more attributions where they discuss instances of actual positive outcomes, whereas engineers in the UK make as many attributions where the positive outcome is seen to be something hypothetical or likely to happen in the future as they do attributions for actual positive outcomes. Thus it would appear that the UK engineers are much more likely to perceive the Change Programme as being yet to produce positive culture change.

These attributions can be broken down still further by looking at the extent to which they have Stable and Global causes. Figure 4.2 illustrates the proportion of attributions that are coded Stable or Global where the Agent is the Change Programme and the outcome is Positive.

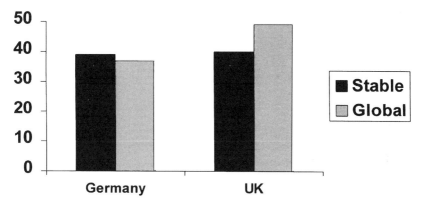

Figure 4.2 Positive attributions: Agent = Change programme

While German and UK engineers attributed similar levels of stability (approximately 40%) to the causes of these positive outcomes, UK engineers perceived the causes to be more Global (50%) than did the German engineers (35%). This would seem to suggest that the UK engineers were more likely to perceive the change programme as having an influence throughout the Company. German engineers, on the other hand, described it as having a more limited influence upon specific individuals or groups.

In comparison we can also look at the attributions that these two groups produced for outcomes caused by the Company. As a whole, both groups of engineers were more likely to perceive the Company as causing negative (73.8%) rather than positive (26.2%) Actual outcomes. Nevertheless, overall, attributions for Hypothetical events were more positive (61.5%) than negative (38.5%). Those attributions where the Company was perceived as having caused a negative outcome were isolated and those attributions produced by German engineers compared with attributions produced by UK engineers (Figure 4.3).

Figure 4.3 clearly illustrates that both groups of engineers perceived the causes of these attributions to be mostly Global (85%). Perhaps not surprising, given that the company (including senior management) has the power and responsibility to influence outcomes at this level. However, the German engineers were more likely to attribute these outcomes to Stable

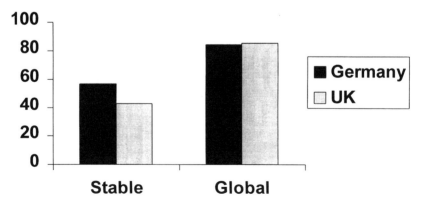

Figure 4.3   Negative attributions: Agent = Company

causes (58%) than the UK engineers (45%) suggesting that the German engineers perceived these negative outcomes to be more permanent than did the UK engineers.

Although this study was based on interviews with a relatively small number of participants, one can see that there were still a substantial number of causal attributions generated. By coding the attributions using the LACS, comparing patterns of attributions produced by engineers in the two countries was possible. Furthermore, certain differences in how these engineers perceived the culture-change programme and the company were detected. It would be tempting to suggest that these differences point to cultural differences between the two groups based upon their membership of different national cultures. For example, according to Hofstede (1991), Germany and the UK differ on two cultural dimensions, those of 'Individualism' and 'Uncertainty Avoidance'. The UK scores higher than Germany on Individualism, one aspect of which is described in terms of a 'willingness to speak one's mind' (Hofstede, 1991, p. 63). The finding that UK engineers were more likely to make negative attributions than their German counterparts may relate, in part, to their higher scores on Individualism. It may also go some way to explain the general perception that UK employees are often willing to complain!

However, comparing attributions produced by individuals in different national divisions of the same international company does not provide a simple comparison of national cultural differences. Differences may also result from the existence of different organisational subcultures stemming from the different experiences of engineers in each national division. In this study, we were interested simply in identifying possible differences in the causal attributions produced by the two groups of engineers. A much larger cross-national study would be required to explore organisational and national differences in attributions separately.

LIMITATIONS TO USING THE METHOD IN THE WORK CONTEXT

The main drawback to using attributional coding is the length of time involved in extracting and coding attributions. If attributional coding is commissioned as part of a project for an organisation, it is worth stressing to the company in advance why the project will take longer than, for example, a questionnaire survey. In my experience, once companies have received a report outlining the results and can see at first hand the rich information that can be gathered from attributional analysis, they are more than willing to accept the timescale. As the practitioner, however, not underestimating the time involved is important—particularly if one is new to the method (it does get easier!).

If one is in a position of having to convince an organisation either to allow access to employees, or to commission a project, it may be worth making the following points. First, attributional coding is not simply a series of interviews followed by a subjective extraction of what the researcher considers to be the main issues. It involves the extraction and objective coding of possibly thousands of individual causal statements. As these statements are then coded individually on different causal dimensions, building up a considerable database that permits quantitative analysis and the identification of patterns of causal beliefs typical of particular groups or individuals is possible. Second, attributional analysis acts as a bridge between quantitative and qualitative approaches in that it can involve the quantitative analysis of qualitative material. Stopping after simply extracting causal attributions is possible, of course. Feeding back comments of individual employees (although anonymously) in the form of causal attributions can help to present a powerful argument to an organisation and always appears more user friendly than tables of statistics!

5

Consumer beliefs and behaviours

Commercial organisations are increasingly recognising the need to understand their customers better. As they pursue this objective, they are coming to realise that consumer behaviour is driven by complex processes of attitude, motivation, aspiration, planning and decision making. Along with such realisation comes a recognition that quantitative surveys are at best a blunt instrument and at worst extremely unreliable, while traditional forms of qualitative market research are quite inadequate. Attributional analysis offers a solution through its ability to process unlimited amounts of qualitative data, interpreted through a strong theory. In this chapter we describe several projects carried out by The Psychology Business Ltd (TPB). This company was set up specifically to extend the range of applications of attributional analysis. In its marketing research it has worked to give the customer a greater voice and to ensure that their perspective is given proper weight.

INTRODUCTION

In the past few years a new approach to customers has developed under the label of relationship marketing (Payne, 1998). The emphasis on relationship reflects, and has given an impetus to, the idea that the customer is an active partner in retailing. One form of activity is when customers 'takes their custom elsewhere' and this issue has concentrated relationship marketing on the issue of loyalty. Two findings have contributed to this move: first, the claim that a retailer's 10% best customers account for 90% of the effect of any advertising that the company does and, second, that retaining existing customers has a far greater effect on profitability than attracting new customers to replace those that move on. Unfortunately the main attempts to implement relationship marketing have been in the form of 'loyalty cards'. These do have some advantages; for example, they can be used in a way that differentially rewards the best (highest spending) customers. However, the supermarkets are now finding that most customers who hold their card also have a card for at least one, sometimes four or five, of their competitors. The effect of the 'loyalty' card has been to encourage customers to shop around for the best bonus points and other bargains—in other words, they have reduced loyalty. How can the marketing industry have made this mistake?

The answer has to be that marketers who devised the loyalty schemes were working with much too simple ideas about customers. They also seem not to have taken account of the extensive findings from psychology about the formation and maintenance of relationships. In this chapter we take relationship marketing as our starting point. We show the various ways in which attributional analysis can help companies form genuine productive relationships with their customers that, like all good relationships, work for the benefit of both. In the process we demonstrate how effectively the attributional approach can be integrated with material from psychology more generally.

DIFFERENT SECTORS, DIFFERENT RELATIONSHIPS

Organisations build up beliefs to help them carry out their functions effectively and comfortably. Even organisations whose existence depends entirely on the behaviour of customers will develop priorities for other aspects: the workforce, the shareholders, the board, the founding family, the maintenance staff. Inevitably, some beliefs about customers will be formulated to fit in with other objectives. Eventually myths about 'our customers' may owe more to the structure and culture of the business than to reliable information about these diverse people.

Certainly the finer points of their beliefs and the determinants of their purchasing behaviour may be lost. Let us consider some examples from different sectors.

Banking and insurance

A major mystery for the financial services sector is why so many people fail to search out and move to cheaper products. It is said that, in Britain, one is more likely to divorce one's spouse than one's bank manager during a lifetime. Is this because of a perceived relationship? Is it because customers have so little trust that they do not believe promises of saving money? Maybe it is a result of what is coming to be called 'confusion marketing' which may keep the customer with the 'devil they know' in banking. However, in newer areas like mobile phones 'confusion marketing' may leave customers so unable to make a rational decision that the market is shared randomly among all the suppliers. Having research that will answer these questions is important but traditional forms may fail to deliver. Do you think anything useful would come from a survey that asked you:

Do you feel you have a relationship with your insurance company?

Or by a few focus groups around the question:

If your bank manager was your lover, what kind of affair would you be having?

Industry needs better research methods and they need to be designed to analyse relationships—or the lack of them.

The next question is: who is the relationship with? The personal insurance industry provides a good example in which the customer's point of direct contact may be the company, a broker, or a call centre. Which relationship are we talking about?

Health

Let us go to the opposite end of insurance's concerns and look at the health industry. Pharmaceutical companies may also have problems identifying the customer with whom they should have a relationship. Traditionally they have seen their customer as the family doctor or the hospital consultant. Increasingly, patients are demanding a say in their own treatment and exerting influence on a medical profession that sees a need to satisfy them. This puts the company in a difficult position: is it to form a relationship with the patients over the head of their doctor? Will the doctor be happy to be seen to have a cosy relationship with the drug company? Non-profit utilities may be moving against the trend. While industry is seeking a more direct relationship with the customer, at least some public services such as the National Health Service have accepted to work in a monetarist framework and to concentrate much attention on the purchaser–provider relationship.

Utilities

Profit utilities, such as electricity, water and gas companies, are also often in a near monopoly position, and are providing something essential to life. Here, without question, the customer is in fact dependent. In such situations it becomes even more crucial to build a relationship. How do customers judge their relationship? The company will have a policy of customer communications and is likely to pay great attention to the normal points of contact: billing, procedures to deal with enquiries, a call centre. However, the staff in these positions get their ideas of relationships from further back in the organisation. It is no use having friendly voices on the telephone if the staff do not believe that promises of services will be kept, or if they know that the culture is one of letting out as little information as possible. Furthermore, staff are members of the local community and, in this respect, perhaps by being customers of their own utility, will have contact with other customers. The relationship therefore must be real and work from deep within the organisation, right out to the full range of customers. We shall discuss this deceptively simple idea of 'a real relationship' later.

Current definitions of quality management break down a manufacturing process into steps in which each department is the customer for what the preceding section has done. Quality is defined in terms of totally meeting the needs of the group defined as the customer for the next stage. Here we see another reason why the idea of relationship marketing must be extended backwards into the organisation. It is not just the interface between the company and the customer that must be bridged by understanding and trust. Interfaces between sections within the company will also benefit from the idea of fostering a relationship.

Retailing

Retailing raises most issues about the participants in the relationship. Do customers relate to the retailer, the brand, or the product? Might they be creating their own entities such as 'medium sized supermarkets' as a focus for their affections? To what extent is it necessary, useful, or damaging that supermarkets and brands compete for these relationships? One consequence of loyalty cards is that stores can now collect extensive information about what each customer buys. They can then use this information to target direct mail, phone calls and other contacts to fit in with the preferences of each individual customer. However, what is it like to be on the receiving end of such a 'relationship'? Could there be, even slightly, the same feeling that someone gets from the attentions of a stalker? Someone out there is watching me, gathering information about me, and then using it. Maybe, with their computer information, they know things about me that I have not even realised about myself.

The point we have reached in this discussion is that if companies want to build relationships with customers they need to think carefully about the kind of relationship towards which they are working. In particular, they need to think through how the relationship looks from the point of view of the customer. Freud's notion of *transference* still holds: that we import into any new relationship what we have learned from similar relationships in the past. Even if companies do not recognise the kind of relationship they are marketing, their customers will, and will respond accordingly. As in any other relationship, customers will make attributions about the intentions of the company, and will base their expectations and responses on these attributions. To gain a full appreciation of what attributional analysis can offer, we will briefly review what psychology has discovered about relationship formation.

WHAT IS A RELATIONSHIP?

What characteristic of a series of interactions make people construe it as a relationship that they value? Spending a little time to see what psychology has to offer on this topic will be worth while before seeing how we have converted all these ideas into practice.

The kind of relationship we know most about is the attachment between mothers and babies. Attachment theory deals with two-way relationships. It has an interesting parallel with changes in marketing because it, too, started life as a theory of dependency, focusing on the one-way transaction in which the mother provides what the baby needs. The company that attempts to increase a market share by making its customers totally dependent is heading for as much disaster as the mother who thinks she can completely control her baby through its dependence on what she provides. Customers, like babies, want empowerment and will fight any situation that limits their choice and renders them powerless.

The term 'attachment' was introduced as an alternative to 'dependency' (e.g. Gewirtz, 1972), to carry the idea of the quality of a two-way relationship. Customers must be enabled to see their relationship in this form. Attachment theory offers many ideas and implications for relationship marketing, but in this chapter we must restrict ourselves to a few of the most important themes.

Our fundamental theme comes from infancy research that shows that the perception of contingencies is fundamental to the formation of attachments. This finding puts attributions at the centre of relationship formation. It is the perception of yourself as cause of the other's behaviour, and vice-versa, that establishes and develops the relationship. Attachment theory, even as originally formulated by John Bowlby (1969) goes further. He described the role of the internal models we have of each other, and of the relationships we perceive between people. Attributional analysis was devised specifically to be able to analyse these internal models. As we explained in Chapter 2, by coding the agent and target in each attribution, we can identify the people involved in each piece of interaction.

Although much of the information about attachments comes from research with children, attachment theory has been found to apply equally to adult relationships. We want you, the reader, at this stage to make a leap of imagination. Imagine that you have just met someone for the first time, and a mutual attraction seems to have developed. Think for a moment about how you would decide that this is a relationship. If it is, how did this happen? And we are practical people, so an additional question might arise: how can I strengthen this relationship?

We can use an understanding of personal relationships in a very detailed way to help understand how relationships with customers can be developed and strengthened. Marketers already talk about customers being loyal or promiscuous, so we are already drawing parallels. Let me take one example of a more detailed comparison. It is said that 95% of all new confectionery products fail when first marketed. What would it say about a relationship between a couple if she only liked one out of every 20 presents he bought her? We would be likely to conclude that he really does not understand her very well. What kind of relationship would survive these continual disappointments?

HOW DO RELATIONSHIPS COME ABOUT?

Summarising many empirical studies of how relationships are formed, we can offer a few general principles. These findings can be used to extend the basic principle that attributions about mutual contingencies are the basis for any perception of a relationship.

Basic requirements

Attractive and accessible

Decades of research with adolescent couples have established beyond all reasonable doubt the simplistic notion that dating is based, first, on whether the other is felt to be physically attractive. The second, equally simple, factor in dating is that the person lives nearby and can be reached easily. We should apply these findings when thinking about marketing a product. Whether this translates into attractive packaging for the brand or a need for the Chairman to be seen as principled, competent and accessible (and good looking), depends on how the relationship is specified.

Each feels the other to be appropriate

Not too grand, not offering too little. One version of this is 'exchange theory' which suggests that people do not want to be over-advantaged or under-advantaged in a relationship. A company that despises or is in awe of its customers or business clients will never strike the right note for a relationship. Customers may use a company that they despise or are made uncomfortable by, but they will be no more loyal than they have to be. This is a subtle factor, to do with a match between self-perceptions and perceptions of the other. It also requires the relationship to be conducted at an appropriate level of intensity.

Each party meets the other's needs

This aspect is rather obvious but needs to be thought of in relation to the others. Attention is more easily captured by things that meet your real or imagined needs, and you are more likely to notice contingent events if they are significant for you. This should be an area that consumer products can deal with easily, but, even here, a simplistic notion of the customer can be damaging. The whole point of commercial pricing is to find the finest possible balance between price and how much people want the product. But this amounts to minimising the overall benefit to the customer and so works against this fundamental aspect of a relationship. One solution is to use the variations in attributing caused by timing: the cost–benefit balance is closest at the point of planning and purchase, whether we are talking about a mother buying beans or a company commissioning market research. The balance should tip towards a perception of needs met at the point of consumption—for example, when the children enjoy the beans in front of the TV. The judgement about when to emphasise a brand's identity must be made in relation to knowledge. Specifically, knowledge about customers' decision making and consumption, and the circumstances in which the product gives satisfaction.

The other provides interesting variations

Interest is strongest in those events that offer 'moderate discrepancies' from the familiar. This is a powerful principle to get beyond the scenario of familiarity leading to boredom. It works both ways and creates problems in two directions. Customers need to be interested by variety, yet they may not want the product to change, and they have little reason to be interested in the workings of the company. Telling them how complex the manufacturing or accounting process has become will not excite them. Reciprocally, the company needs to recognise the complexity and changeability of its customers. The variety is certainly there, but is often underestimated by marketers, let alone by boards of directors. Nevertheless, to try to have a relationship with a simplified stereotype of customers and not to be curious to learn more about them is a recipe for failure.

Each has an expectation of influencing, and being influenced by, the other

This is the fundamental and most complex factor in developing a relationship, already mentioned when we were discussing attachment (above). We are biologically designed to notice when someone (or something) is responsive to us. Technically, we are attuned to events that are contingent on our own behaviours. We do not merely notice contingent events. We enjoy them. So even babies get pleasure from noticing that when they throw the toy out of the cot someone immediately returns it. Specifically, each partner must feel that he or she is influencing the other. An experiment to illustrate this would be to cut off all response during a conversation—for example, to turn your back to the person who is talking. That person will find it very disconcerting, and difficult to continue. Do not try this at home.

It is the attribution that you cause the other's behaviour, and vice-versa, that establishes and develops the relationship. This factor poses challenges for companies that must be seen to be responsive and yet must make decisions based on commercial or other considerations that may conflict with the motivations of customers. Nevertheless, somehow the customers must feel that the company is working to give them what they need. The only solution here is to know what the customers need in such detail that there are ample options opened up and a reliable fit can be achieved. Relationship marketing has approached this issue largely through data on past purchasing activity. Obviously, this can only tell how the customers have responded to what has been on offer in the past. It is less likely to be effective in suggesting novel strategies or products that might make customers feel that their changing needs are being precisely met, or in making them feel actively involved in the relationship.

Other useful areas of psychology

We have restricted this review to well-established findings about relationships, but there are plenty of other psychological principles relevant to relationship marketing. For example:

- Maslow's hierarchy of needs, which can be used to predict factors that will determine whether the needs a product can meet are relevant to the customer at that time.
- Social referencing, which is the phenomenon that people judge the appropriateness of their response by what they think others would do.
- Social identity theory (Tajfel, 1982), which has much to say about how people define themselves in relation to the groups with which they identify.

Taken together, these principles all point to a need to know the customers in detail, and then to be able to respond to them in ways they will recognise. Not quite 'to know them is to love them', but not so far off. In our opinion the research tools available to marketers have not always had the capacity to provide the information needed to build a relationship. The requirements are not just for depth of information, but for an understanding of how the customers construe the brand, product or company in relation to their lifestyle and values. Then we need to know how they go about their decisions to act, which is a more difficult question than just knowing what they approve of. Finally, we need to be able to analyse the company in the same terms as their customers to enable areas of synergy and areas of conflict to be identified.

APPLICATIONS OF THE LEEDS ATTRIBUTIONAL CODING SYSTEM

As a research company The Psychology Business (TPB) has the opportunity, within the limits of confidentiality, to review research in a wide range of sectors, linked by the fact that all were based in attributional analysis. Because the methods for attributional research were developed in the context of family therapy, they naturally reflect the need to deal with relationships. Here we show how they have been adapted to work in marketing. As a summary, the attributional researcher can:

- use a system of interviewing (in our case derived from systemic family therapy) to elicit a detailed commentary about individuals' expectations of their own thoughts, feelings and behaviours and those of significant others;
- pull together repeated aspects of the thinking of those individuals, even if expressed in a series of partial statements in no fixed order;
- develop a method of tabulating the data that can deal with any level of complexity and quantity of data;
- ensure that the analysis of the data is rooted in perceptions of cause and contingency.

Fundamentally, the research method operates through the following sequence:

(1) generating high-quality verbatim descriptions from individuals or groups;
(2) tabulating all expressions of causal belief (attributions);
(3) identifying the people, products and other entities involved in each attribution;

(4) coding the five standard 'dimensions' of each cause, sepa-
     rately for the speaker, the identified agent and the identi-
     fied target, where applicable;
(5) coding contextual information;
(6) processing the coded attributions in great detail to be able
     to summarise the patterns of belief and choices of action of
     the consumers;
(7) using psychological theory and findings to convert the at-
     tributional findings into practical suggestions for action.

Typically, 50 interviews (stage 1) will generate 15,000 attributional statements (stage 2), each of which will be coded for
speaker, agent and target (stage 3) and then the five attributional
dimensions are coded as described in Chapter 2 (stage 4). The
major extension of the LACS for marketing research is an extensive content coding (stage 5). We may use up to 24 headings, with
anything from 2 to 80 items to choose from for each heading. This
data set is then analysed in great detail to determine the concerns,
values and sources of action of the respondents (stage 6). Because
the method will handle any amount of data, it extends the scope
of qualitative research to a point at which, with careful recruiting,
the sample size allows generalisation of findings to the wider
group of representative customers. Usually the analysis generates
a model of consumer decision processes which can be interpreted
from the psychological processes involved to give clear and explicit guidelines for action (stage 7).

    The remainder of this chapter is devoted to describing applica-
tions of the method by TPB in three consumer areas. In some cases
certain details have been changed to preserve confidentiality.
However, the first two examples have already been published in
some detail as examples of the methodology, so we can identify the
companies, and you can follow them up if you wish.

The radio station: investigating a marketing relationship in different cultures

This project shows how the LACS methodology can be applied to
make comparisons across different cultures and with data col-
lected in different languages. It was also one of the first in which

the qualitative methodology of LACS provided a base from which to derive a set of questions for use in a quantitative survey.

The relationship between a broadcaster and the audience becomes ever more crucial as choice widens. Much of the world's population depends on international radio for reliable information and a wider perspective. We have found that regular listeners come to feel that they have a personal relationship with their favourite station and with its regular presenters. Sponsors of International Broadcasting require evidence to support the claim that the relationship built up by the station conveys a feeling of quality of a kind that will then become associated with the country of origin. To test the claim, TPB was commissioned by the BBC to develop a Performance Indicator with fairly stringent requirements. It had to be based in the framework of thinking and motivation of International Broadcast listeners and reflect their judgements of what, for them, constituted quality. It should apply across the great range of countries to which the World Service broadcasts, allowing comparisons to be made, but also be sensitive to cultural and other variations between the countries. It had to apply equally to all International Broadcasters, and to generate survey questions by which the performance of the World Service and its competitors could be tracked. In meeting these objectives we have built a concept of what constitutes effective quality (Stratton, 1995a). We have also developed a database that is a rich source of material for answering questions about the way that style and content can be adjusted to sustain and develop the relationship with listeners.

In each country we train an interviewer and run between 6 and 12 discussion groups of listeners. The recordings are processed by a native language speaker to identify every statement in which an identifiable event is explained with an explicit cause. Typically a 90-minute group will generate 250 of these attributional statements. The process of extracting the attributions is, where possible, carried out in the original language, preferably by the interviewer. In this way we avoid imposing our own cultural assumptions about how causal beliefs are expressed. Having been identified within the language and frame of reference of the country, the attributions are then translated and entered into a computer database for coding.

In the process of developing the performance indicator of audience perception of quality, we have so far conducted group discussions in 15 countries. In all, about 1,000 listeners to international radio broadcasting have provided some 44,000 attributional statements. The coding has three components. The first identifies the people involved in each attribution. Let us take an example:

Because the BBC gives the news immediately, my friends always know what is going on.

The cause here comes from the BBC which is therefore identified as the agent. The outcome affects the speaker's friends, who are therefore the target. From this statement we have information about how the speaker sees the relationship between the broadcaster and the speaker's friends. By combining statements that apply to different combinations of people we can build up a comprehensive account of all the different relationships.

The second stage of coding is to identify in some detail the content of each statement. Some of the headings for the content index were:

- The station being referred to
- Values
- Programme content
- Timing
- Actions taken
- Evaluation.

For the example above: the station involved is the BBC; a value in the cause is speed and in the outcome is knowledge. Programme content is news; the reference is to the present but applies to past and future; the action in the cause is broadcasting but no action is specified in the outcome. Both cause and outcome refer to something that is approved and exists (rather than being wished for). In all, 12 content codes, each with up to 60 categories, were assigned to each attribution.

The final stage of coding is to rate the standard set of attributional dimensions for the statement. In the example, the cause is stable (will apply into the future) and global (is about something with wide significance for the people under consideration). This combination of dimensions applied to a media service identifies aspects that are intrinsic to that provider.

From the perspective of the targets, the attribution is personal (it differentiates them from other people) and controllable (they can influence how much they know what is going on). Significant statements that are personal and indicate control relate to empowerment for the people involved.

Consistently, across all the 15 countries we have surveyed, we found that values which rate highly on '*intrinsic*' identify aspects of the station of which the listener approves or disapproves. Values associated with '*empowerment*' are more consistently related to whether or not the person listens to that station.

A station will need to be perceived positively in both respects to achieve a good relationship with its audience in terms of positive perception, consistent use, and audience loyalty. To be valued for intrinsic quality, but not to offer empowerment, will mean that the broadcaster is admired and respected but not listened to. Empowerment without intrinsic value means that the station is used but not respected or valued and so will be readily discarded. Again we can apply these ideas to an interpersonal relationship. Being admired from afar is very pleasant but not of much practical use for a relationship. Being extremely useful but not liked or respected is not a relationship we would want either. For an international broadcaster with a brief to represent the home culture positively, being rated highly on both intrinsic and empowering aspects is essential. We have summarised the combination of the two sets of values as '*effective quality*'. The next task was to determine the components of effective quality, and to identify how they operated.

Within the analysis, it was possible to identify, and scale, the values that contributed to perceptions of intrinsic value and empowerment. Those values that contributed to both aspects were selected, and the coding of statements making up each value was intensively analysed to determine which values operated similarly in attributional terms, and so could be grouped together. From this stage of the analysis emerged six core values that accounted for the majority of variation in the data. These core values represented the key components of effective quality and then became the basis for subsequent analyses.

The data from the 15 different countries, independently analysed, consistently generated the same four dominant core
values, with four others that operated occasionally. There were
also substantial variations between countries in which core
values were most important, and in the relative significance of
the values in contributing to effective quality.

Six typical core values are listed in Table 5.1. It is important to
recognise that what we are offering are summary labels and
definitions which best capture the range of meaning of each
value. The words we have chosen will rarely have been used by
the respondents.

Each core value is evaluated in terms of its relative strength on
a variety of indicators. Some of these derive from how frequently components of the value were present in causal attributions. Others derived from the tendency for the attributions to
fall into certain significant patterns. Because the data consist of
many coded statements, assigning relative weights to these different aspects is possible. In particular, the two essential components of 'intrinsic' and 'empowering' are weighted separately
for each core value, in terms of salience in the discussion (measured by frequency of reference) and attributional power. The
latter is measured by the extent to which the specified attributional pattern exceeds the statistically expected level.

TABLE 5.1   Six core values of international broadcasting

Value	Summary definition
Functional	Does the essential aspects of the job well. Includes professionalism and production values
Informative	Effectively transmits the important information
Credible	Can be trusted to be objective and accurate
Empathetic	Understands and respects the values of the local culture and works to make its material accessible
Interesting	Presents intrinsically interesting material in an engaging form
Distinctive	Has a recognisable style and a clear and acceptable identity

The six core values, and the relative weightings attached to each aspect of each of them, constitute a mathematical model of effective quality. The data within each location are used to quantify the components of the model so that each aspect of the audience perception of effective quality can be independently specified. Questions for a survey in each country are then derived from the attributional analysis. Each question is derived from a detailed specification provided by the attributional analysis. We use the scoring of each value in terms of how it is seen as intrinsic to a broadcaster; the kind of empowerment it provides; the degree to which it is seen positively or negatively; the dominant pattern of attributional dimensions associated with the value; the context within which the value most often operates; and, finally, the wording used by respondents in typical references. The questionnaire is therefore closely specified to incorporate the most important values for that country in the form that listeners most often think about them.

All of the values in effective quality combine a perception of the intrinsic qualities of the station which determine the level of approval, and of the empowering aspects which indicate the effect on that person's life. They provide a clear definition of the felt relationship with the broadcaster. From this point we can go on to identify the strengths and weaknesses of the relationship with the audience in each country; to find better ways of defining subgroups within the audience; and to examine individual programmes and presenters to assess the ways in which they contribute to, or detract from, different aspects of the relationship.

The airline: meeting each others' needs through reciprocal interaction

A second example comes from another study published in some detail (Stratton, 1991, 1997). An early commercial application of attributional analysis was to long-haul passengers flying economy with British Airways. The amount of raw data available was limited because we used recordings from three focus groups that had not been run with attributional analysis in mind. However, it is a strength of the LACS method that it can be applied to most kinds of verbatim material. Here the method could identify quite complex patterns in the thinking of passengers, and could derive very concrete recommendations from them.

Personnel

For the coding of agent and target, we concentrate on people if any are mentioned. Consequently, our index had various kinds of people, and a few other essential categories: respondents themselves, passengers in general, and cabin crew were the most significant. The airline was mentioned sometimes, and the quality of service also figured. Apart from these, food and drink seemed very much on the minds of passengers. Altogether 234 (out of 1,039) attributions were made in which food and drink were mentioned.

Much can be learned from the simple question of how often different people feature as agents or targets in attributions. The frequencies are shown in Table 5.2. One can see that respondents, and passengers in general, were much more likely to be targets (648 times) than agents (153 times). In other words, respondents and passengers in general were much more often seen as experiencing the consequences of a causal sequence than initiating it. Although the crew were more often agents than targets, the high figure for targets suggests much interest in the

TABLE 5.2   Frequency of attributions for agent and target

Agent	Target					
	Respon-dent	Pas-senger	Crew	Quality factor	Air-line	Total
Respondent	35	0	7	1	2	50
Passenger	3	33	36	6	3	103
Crew	27	141	65	3	2	240
Quality factor	20	99	13	3	2	147
Airline	10	23	20	7	1	83
Total	176	472	181	64	19	1,039

influences on their behaviour as well as in the effects they have. Most of the interest in the airline concerned the effects it had: the airline featured as an agent more than four times as often as it did a target.

Comparing the frequencies with which given agents affect different targets begins to suggest how the relationships work. For example, crew affect passengers 141 times, whereas passengers affect the crew only 36 times. Other agent–target comparisons in Table 5.2 show how informative this coding can be even before the attributional dimensions are interpreted.

Attribution coding

One thousand and thirty-nine statements were coded for all five of the attributional dimensions. As this research was exploratory, we had no basis for selecting some dimensions over others.

To show how one attributional dimension was used in relation to coding people involved as agents and targets, Figure 5.1 shows the percentage of statements for each kind of agent in which that agent had control. Attributional analysis can rapidly get to a level of complexity that is confusing, so it may help to unpack that statement. We are not calculating the proportion of

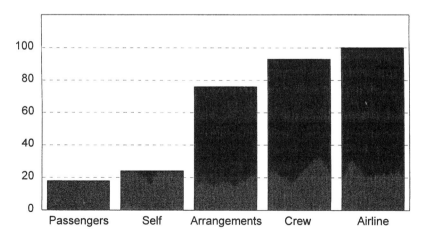

Figure 5.1 Amount of control (%)

statements during the interviews that implied control by each type of person. We take, for each category (passengers, crew, etc.), all the attributions in which that person was an agent. We then see how many of those statements were of a kind that apportioned control to that person. For example:

People want two drinks with their meal, you shouldn't have to ask for them.

or more generally:

When the customer has particular needs, the hostess should be sensitive to them.

In these two attributions the 'passenger' is the agent, but has no control over the outcome. Control is, according to these attributions, in the hands of the airline hostess or steward. In contrast, consider the following attribution:

British Airways have good training programmes so you get competent service.

Here the agent is the airline, and the outcome is very much under its control.

From Figure 5.1 we can see that passengers are rarely seen as in control of events. As often happens, respondents saw themselves as having a little more control than passengers in general. It is a very common tendency for the worst complaints to be made, and the worst situations to be described, on behalf of some general class of people rather than the speakers themselves. At the other end of the continuum, cabin crew are seen as highly likely to be able to influence the events in which they are involved. Strikingly, every statement in which British Airways was identified as the agent in the cause presented the airline as having some control over the outcome.

Content coding

Setting up an index to code aspects of each statement is very easy. For example, in this study we coded the cause and the outcome separately for each statement in terms of the provision or resource being described. Items were:

- physical need
- psychological need;
- physical or psychological state other than a need;
- standard in-flight facility or factor;
- standard out-flight facility or factor;
- special service (beyond what is basic and paid for);
- practicalities.

Each item is accompanied by a brief definition and examples to ensure consistency between coders, and an acceptable level of reliability. For example, physical need was defined as 'mention of any requirement to do with bodily functions, sustenance, physical comfort (e.g. seating, air quality), and physical safety'.

Some content codes apply to the attributional statement as a whole. Because the distinction between positive and negative outcomes is so important in attribution theory, an indicator of overall positive or negative evaluation is often used. A further coding used in this study was whether the attribution suggested a met, or unmet need. The categories we used are shown in the report of overall frequency of the categories used during the interviews (Figure 5.2). Evidently, using ratios of attributions falling into different categories can provide useful insights into the relative emphasis given to different concerns. 'Essential

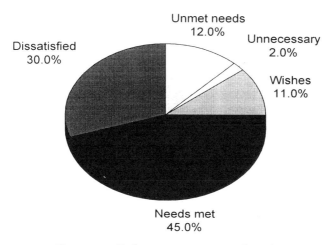

Figure 5.2   References to meeting of needs

requirements' are not discussed frequently, but taken for granted, and are rarely said to be missing. However, unwanted features and events are often referred to.

An airline manager looking at these results may want to know more: How does my airline compare with the general figures for satisfaction in Figure 5.2? What kinds of needs are met by standard care and what kind by special care? What are the implications of the low level of control experienced by passengers? Such questions are answered by the detailed exploration of data prescribed by the grounded theory approach. It is this process that takes attributional analysis beyond a simple quantification of content coding.

The exploratory analysis

The basic analysis described so far provided some important pointers to issues that concern passengers. First is a disturbing lack of perceived control. It is probably significant that the tendency to uncontrollability is more strongly attributed to passengers in general than to the respondents themselves. People will often attribute more disturbing or unacceptable thoughts to the population in general so that they do not have to complain about, take the blame for, or be seen to be not coping with such thoughts themselves.

The frequency of uncontrollable attributions even when they are agents must be interpreted in relation to the fact that passengers are more than four times as often targets than they are agents. Meanwhile the crew and the airline have the opposite pattern attributed to them, being very much in control. Together, these findings suggest a considerable dependency felt by the passengers.

A high level of dissatisfaction is also evident (Figure 5.2). However, dissatisfaction, and suggestions for dealing with it, are not about essential requirements such as safety but about mundane provisions. Examples include constant supply of mineral water, games to stave off boredom, the possibility of walking around and talking to the crew and, above all, better food, more food, less food, different food, and special food. The same comments applied to the availability of drink.

The analysis so far led us to the idea that long-haul flights induce a powerful sense of relinquishing control, even over life and death, to the airline and its staff. Passengers then try to deal with this anxiety by demanding to be looked after. They feel that if they are cosseted, fed, and generally cared for, they would have greater confidence that the airline and staff had their best interests at heart. This confidence could then be extended to essential requirements such as safety that are too frightening to question directly. (Several people talked about anxiety and fear but none ever questioned the safety of the plane.) We formulated this hypothesis in relation to attachment theory and the idea that passengers were seeking evidence that they were provided with a 'secure base' (Bowlby, 1988).

Once the hypothesis was formed and checked out in the data, we started to realise just what a dilemma the airline was in. Apart from the extra cost that would be involved in providing what passengers were asking for, British Airways was caught in a paradox. The more it responded to these expressed needs, the more it moved towards making the passenger dependent on the crew for every aspect of their functioning. So just providing what was asked for could make the underlying problem of helplessness worse. This dilemma provided a focus for one aspect of the more intensive analysis of the data. It is that aspect that we will follow through in more detail.

Attributional patterns

Once attribution dimensions have been coded, as described in Chapter 2, they can be analysed individually (as above) or taken in combination. From the perspective of the passenger the most common pattern was:

Stable—global—external—universal—uncontrollable

This pattern occurred in 363 out of 1,039 attributions. Using our standard coding format, allocating '1' for stable, '0' for unstable, etc., this pattern can be represented numerically as 11000. Any pattern of the five attributional dimensions can be expressed as a five-digit binary number of this kind, which gives us a useful shorthand for referring to different patterns.

The 11000 pattern refers to important causes (they will recur and they have significant consequences). However, they originate outside the respondent, do not identify the respondent as a unique individual in any way, and are not easily influenced by the respondent. Such statements do not involve the respondent. They are someone else's business. In the BBC study respondents used this pattern when identifying aspects of the broadcaster that were important, but not of direct concern to the listener.

The frequencies with which this pattern applied to different kinds of outcome are given in Figure 5.3. For this kind of analysis it is possible to compute the expected value, statistically speaking, of the frequency. Expected frequencies tell us something about the frequencies one might expect to see purely based on chance. The procedure uses the overall frequencies in the way that a chi-square calculation works out an expected value. So, for example, although psychological needs were outcomes in 36 attributions, we would have expected a figure of 61 occurrences based on the frequency with which this factor was discussed.

Figure 5.3 shows that the 11000 pattern most commonly applies to 'special service'. The reported frequency is above what has been predicted statistically, even given the great importance

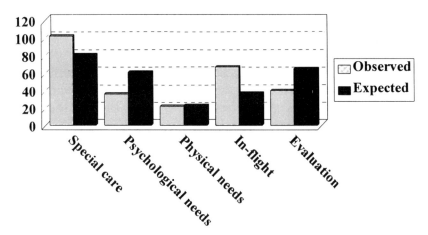

Figure 5.3 Attributions to the form stable, global, external, universal, uncontrollable

attached to this type of outcome. Because 'special service' refers to a special degree of being looked after, its prevalence with the 11000 pattern is highly significant. Factors leading to special service are regarded as important and likely to continue to operate. However, the respondents feel that they have no involvement in the way in which this kind of service comes about, and that it is not geared to them personally.

The pattern next most strongly associated with special service is 11010 (stable, global, external, personal, uncontrollable). This differs from the previous pattern because an element of individuality of the respondent is involved. Here psychological needs and evaluation also occurred at above the predicted level. It seems that where psychological needs such as relaxation are concerned, respondents are much more aware of their own specific requirements. However, they still see the identified causal factors as external to them and outside their control.

Much of the research on attributional style has concentrated on the 11110 (stable, global, internal, personal, uncontrollable) pattern. Such events are important, and are seen as arising from, and being unique to, the individual. However, they are not under the person's control. Clinically, such a pattern (when causes of things going wrong are consistently attributed in this way) is associated with depression (see Chapter 3). In the British Airways data the pattern is rare, as might be expected (22 instances), but the most common association is with the psychological needs.

In all, nine different patterns of attributing were identified as occurring with significant frequency. What is striking is that every one of these patterns ends with the respondent not being in control of the outcome. The respondents did exert control in some areas, but from this analysis such instances were clearly inconsistent, i.e. were not associated with any particular kind of causal sequence.

Special care

The high frequency of special care in the significant (and common) attributional pattern of 11000 led us to explore this issue in

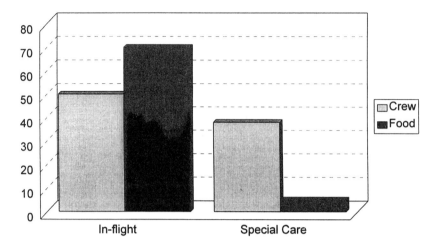

Figure 5.4   Routine in-flight provision versus special care

more detail. One comparison (in Figure 5.4) is whether the crew, or the provision of food and drink, dominates as a source of special service and of standard in-flight provision.

While food and drink predominate in perceptions of standard provision, special service is seen as coming almost exclusively from the crew. This reliance on the crew for special care was consistent throughout the analyses. Figure 5.5 shows that, although some satisfaction with the special care provided is evident, significant dissatisfaction was also expressed.

The analysis then turned to the finding that psychological needs dominate in relation to special service. When special service was a cause, 25% of the outcomes related to psychological needs, but none related to physical needs. Also, the strongest expressions of dissatisfaction were associated with psychological needs (10%) but never with physical needs. Finally, of the 34% of attributions in which crew were agents and the outcome was some form of special service (either provided or not provided), 29% of these cases related to psychological needs. However, only 3% related to physical needs, and 5% to standard in-flight provision.

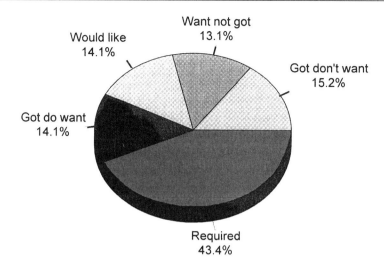

Figure 5.5   Levels of satisfaction with special care

Application of numerical data to the original attributional statements

The final phase in the analysis, before deriving our recommendations, was to use significant tendencies in the data to identify groups of statements. At this point a statistical package or spreadsheet, including the numerical coding and the text of each attribution, becomes useful. Figure 5.6 lists some attributional statements selected for the pattern of attributional dimensions and identified from the content coding as dealing with particular issues.

By exploring the statements in different groups, it becomes possible to formulate a description of the range of content covered by, for example, attributions coded 11010, in which the cause is a psychological need and the outcome is a requirement for special service. In practice, after the first pass of this stage of the analysis, further hypotheses will be suggested, and other combinations of variables will be checked for their prevalence and significance, as indicated by the dominant attributional patterns associated with them. We return to the statements with a new group until satisfied that all the major patterns have been identified.

```
┌─────────────────────────────────────────────────────────────┐
│ SPECIAL SERVICE                                               │
├─────────────────────────────────────────────────────────────┤
│   If you get into a conversation with staff in the bay area   │
│   it's genuine friendliness                                   │
│                                                               │
│   They don't have to talk to you                              │
│   you feel as if you belong                                   │
│                                                               │
│   You get into a conversation with staff                      │
│   you feel it's a family type of environment                  │
│                                                               │
│   They apologise then bring your drink                        │
│   you think 'she recognises my needs'                         │
│                                                               │
│   If you are treated as an individual                         │
│   it makes you feel like you are a valued customer            │
│                                                               │
│   The stewardess makes an effort with the kids                │
│   you feel she is caring                                      │
├─────────────────────────────────────────────────────────────┤
│ PSYCHOLOGICAL NEEDS                                           │
├─────────────────────────────────────────────────────────────┤
│   You can pick up vibes from the way people look              │
│   crew should be aware of non-verbal communication            │
│                                                               │
│   When you have a problem                                     │
│   the crew should comfort you straight away                   │
│                                                               │
│   If you feel claustrophobic on the plane                     │
│   the crew could offer you a drink                            │
│                                                               │
│   Passengers with a problem                                   │
│   the stewardess should not embarrass them                    │
└─────────────────────────────────────────────────────────────┘
```

Figure 5.6 Sample attributional statements relating to special service and psychological needs

Conclusions, recommendations and evaluation

Only the most important aspects of the analysis have been described here. Other avenues were explored and other themes were identified. However, the findings reported are sufficient to show how we reached our recommendations. In summary, the major themes were of the relationships between the passengers' feelings of handing over control, the requirement for special service, and its association with psychological needs, combined with the particular involvement of cabin crew in providing or failing to provide what was wanted.

Our recommendation to British Airways was that a simple response to the request for special service might be counterproductive. It could very easily be done in a way that would increase the passengers' lack of control, and their dependence on the airline, in which case it would increase their sense of vulnerability. However, it was vulnerability that we felt was driving the need for special service in the first place. We offered a series of action points designed to avoid the potential vicious circle, and to meet the needs suggested in this research without incurring substantial extra costs. The summary action points were as follows:

1. Recognise passengers as individuals.
2. Extend passengers' sense of control where possible. Offer choice during the flight, for example, choice of seating, food, drinks, etc.
3. Explore the kinds of attention to detail and special service that will make passengers feel more individual and better looked after.
4. Train crews to recognise psychological needs and relate them to special levels of care. Emphasise that they, the crew, are the main channel through which these fundamental needs such as reassurance, a sense of individuality, the ability to make a relationship, can be met.
5. By implementing action point 4, allow passengers to feel that they have an appropriate, non-dependent relationship with the crew.
6. Train crews in procedures to ensure that requests are not forgotten
7. Continue to emphasise the airline's total commitment to safety and reliability.

The television company: who responds to direct response TV advertisements?

A different kind of customer-oriented application arose in a study of direct response TV advertisements (DRTAs). The issue was to discover why some viewers make phone calls in response to ads, while most do not. The problem is one of a group in which a kind of decision process takes place. However, it is so quick and relatively unimportant that people have no possibility of reporting their own processes. The approach we took was to use attributional analysis to understand the difference in orientation and attitude of people who responded to those of ordinary viewers. Then we could make recommendations about the factors that would help non-responders to make use of the advertisements (Stratton, 1995b).

The conditions that would produce this kind of change in consumer behaviour may not need to be particularly powerful. What is needed may be quite subtle shifts in perceptions, assumptions, expectations and evaluations. However, such subtle factors present a complex challenge to research. What is needed is not the identification of powerful forces, but an uncovering of those subtle factors that make the difference in whether a person does or does not take action. Responses to DRTAs are probably the kind of situation in which we feel that we want to do something but somehow do not quite manage to do it. The suggestion that the research problem here is similar to that of getting people to take exercise, eat more healthily, give up smoking and phone their in-laws gives some measure of the difficulty of the task.

As part of a major study of the workings of DRTAs, British Telecom and Channel 4 commissioned a qualitative study from TPB. The aim was to find out whether identifying factors that would result in people phoning in response to these advertisements was possible. In relatively uncharted areas such as this we prefer to think in terms of 'co-missioning'—a cooperative and interactive process to give the research the best chance of producing the practical solutions that the client needs.

Procedures

Eight groups each of eight respondents who claimed never to have made a phone call in response to an advertisement on television, participated in 90-minute discussions. Twelve people who had responded to at least one advertisement during the last year participated in 45-minute individual interviews.

The design of the study was specified to provide the broadest range of information. It is in no sense a normative or balanced subject pool, and the total numbers are too small to permit claims of reliable or generalisable findings. The results are presented without qualification to avoid pointless repetition, but interpreting them in the light of the limitations in the sample is essential.

Core issues

Using attributional analysis we found that the full range of values, attitudes and motivations present in the accounts offered by the respondents clustered into five distinct sets. Each of these sets of 'core issues' is made up of a cluster of subordinate values that, in the context of direct response advertising, work in similar ways. Each of the five core issues defines one aspect of the ways that viewers react to DRTAs. Together, and taking account of their relative importance in different contexts, the five core issues provide the basis for a detailed unpacking of the psychological processes elicited in viewers by DRTAs. Figure 5.7 shows the relative strength of the issues.

Each of the core issues is made up of a number of components. The components were clustered together because they operated in the thinking and planning of respondents in consistent ways as indicated by the attributional patterns involved. The issue of 'relevance' is unpacked in detail as an illustration of the

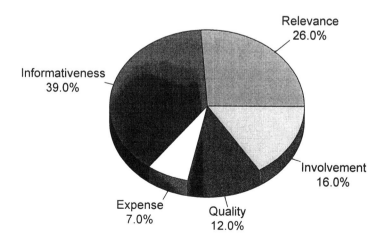

Figure 5.7 Core issues for viewers of direct response television advertisements

information available. Then the remaining core issues are briefly described.

Relevance is composed of six components whose relative importance in the discussions is shown in Figure 5.8.

The core issue of relevance reflects how the direct response advertisement fits in with and is personally relevant to that individual's way of life.

The first consideration is whether the advert causes the viewers to think personally about the information it contains. Equally importantly, the viewers are also considering whether they want the product or service: whether they have a need for it. When we inspected the attributional statements, it was clear that the dominant theme was whether the advertisement taps into some priority of which the viewers are already aware. Only once an interest is established does the issue of whether the product is value for money become significant.

The convenience to the viewers is also an important factor reflected in this core issue. When there is a call to action, the perceived relevance is moderated in terms of the effort or inconvenience involved in following it up. The remaining components are of what choices the viewers have about the product category, and whether the particular item is seen to be personally relevant.

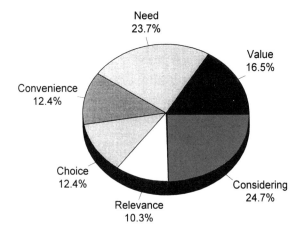

Figure 5.8 Components of the core issue of relevance

The relevance core issue is seen by the viewers as a generally positive or else neutral aspect of adverts. The perception of relevance can be significantly influenced by the style and content of the advertisement. Further insight into the core issue is provided by the dominant aspects of the attributional dimensions.

Relevance is not seen as a fixed feature of an advertisement (unstable), but it does have wide implications for the viewers (global). In these respects it is more relevant to the everyday life of the viewers than is informativeness, whose significance lies in its role during television watching. The degree of relevance is determined by the personal reactions of the viewers, who then perceive themselves as having control and so able to decide what, if any, action to take in relation to it.

The capacity of the viewers to act on relevance, combined with the tendency for relevance to be a function of situation and to be modifiable, makes 'consequences' a crucial aspect of an advertisement. It suggests that relevance is not a fixed quantity—as if an advert will either be relevant to viewers or not. The research indicates that this core issue is weighted slightly more in the attributions of people who have responded to DRTAs, but it is also significant for non-responders. Our overall impression is that it is not lack of personal relevance in the advertisements that prevents non-responders from phoning.

The strongest of the core issues (see Figure 5.7) concerns whether the advertisement provides information for the viewers. Information is valued if it is clear and easily understandable. The issue of informativeness is bound up with whether the DRTA appeals to the viewers: does it please them, does it provoke liking or dislike as something to view? Also important is whether the advert is getting its message across effectively: whether the advert works for the viewers. The negative side of this aspect is advertisements which are confusing. If the viewers have to struggle (in their view unnecessarily) to understand the point the advert is making or perhaps the brand it is promoting, they become resentful.

Informativeness is seen by the viewers as, in general, being a positive aspect of adverts. Reactions in terms of 'informativeness' are reactions to the advertisement as a piece of television. These reactions predominantly indicate a positive attitude to 'advertisements as television'. The research indicates that this core issue is more important to the non-responders than to responders.

The core issue of 'involvement' arouses interest in and draws attention to the advert. Something that might concern a company more than it might concern an advertising agency is that interest is predominantly on the advert itself more than on the product or service advertised. A consideration is whether the advert as a visual stimulus is interesting or perhaps even fascinating. Humour, if present and effective in the advertisement, plays a significant part in a positive judgement on this value.

Like informativeness, interest is seen by the viewers as a positive aspect of adverts. Advertisements which scored highly on this core issue would be perceived by the viewers as making a positive contribution to their television watching. This would be expected to produce a generally favourable attitude to the product, but could lead the viewers away from seeing the advertisement as a reason to make an immediate response. The research indicates that this core issue is a more important issue for the non-responders than for the responders.

The core issue of 'quality' reflects the viewers' concerns about the standards of the advert itself as well as of the product or service being described. The main issue is whether the product or service or company that supplies them are trustworthy. Much of this aspect involved concerns about whether the product or service on offer can be taken at face value or whether the limited information available from a television advertisement is concealing negative aspects.

While the first concern is with the product or service being offered, the viewers then move on to consider aspects of the company such as its stability. At its simplest, a worry about reliability may be a worry about whether the company will still exist in a few months' time should it be necessary to return the item.

This core issue is more likely to be negative than positive. When it is perceived as being an issue, quality is highly significant to the viewers. They do not see their judgements on this as in any way personal—it is entirely an issue about the company and the product. Correspondingly, quality is outside the control of the viewers. So this is a potentially extremely important issue from which they are personally excluded. Also, with the exception of well-known companies, they are entirely dependent for their judgement on the content and style of the advertisement.

The quality issue captures the suspicion that viewers sometimes feel about whether they are exposing themselves to poor value or some other cost by responding to a DRTA. It is likely to work as a gatekeeper, being more often a reason not to respond than a positive incentive to respond. The implication is that an effective DRTA will provide reassurance about either or both the quality of the company, and the quality of the product/service. At the very least it must avoid provoking concerns about the trustworthiness of either the company or its products. Quality was a more important issue to the responders than to non-responders.

'Expense' reflects the viewers' concerns about the financial involvement with direct response advertisements and their companies. It brings together a number of concerns about the potential cost of responding. Whether the viewers will benefit financially, by not having to pay for the phone call for example, or if they will be at a financial disadvantage through involvement with direct response, for example, being persuaded into buying something that they do not want.

Viewers' concerns about excessive costs, such as over-priced products and charges for post and packaging, contribute to this core issue. If expense is consciously considered, the feeling is negative. The attributional pattern is the same as that of quality. When it becomes an issue it is an overriding concern, but not one over which the viewers have any personal influence. Expense therefore operates rather like quality, in being primarily a significant reason for resisting a response if concerns about it are activated by any aspect of the DRTA. As with quality, it is more of an issue for responders than non-responders.

A detailed consideration of the five core issues indicated that there were important respects in which they coalesced further. The values of informativeness and involvement were more consistently associated with simple approval or disapproval, and less often with decisions to take action. They were also more dominant in the thinking of the people who had never responded to a DRTA.

The core issues of relevance, quality and expense were more associated with decisions about whether to act or to make choices. Quality and expense, and to a lesser extent relevance, were more important issues for those people who had in the past responded to DRTAs.

The core issues of informativeness and involvement can be joined to form the value set labelled 'appreciation', a set of values that reflect the viewers' reactions to the direct response advertisements primarily as a piece of television, which may be entertaining, educational or irritating.

The attributional analysis of the issues within appreciation showed that they were seen as relatively permanent aspects, but not having a major impact on the lives of the viewers. The aspects of advertisements that produced appreciation were external to the viewers and they felt that other people would react similarly. While informativeness varied with the advertisement, their involvement was under their own control.

Value statements in the appreciation set are generally positive and likely to be associated with approval. The components of *appreciation* are of a kind that are likely to apply to television viewing overall. Their strength in this research suggests that advertisements are widely seen as a component of general television viewing. The fact that advertisements are generally seen positively in these respects suggests that they are often felt to be contributing to the quality of viewing.

Nothing in the research suggests that the values leading to appreciation are usually dysfunctional for advertisements: this was not an issue that the data could address. However, the way this cluster operates suggests that it might have negative consequences specifically for DRTAs. Tentatively, we suggested that a strong performance on involvement could distract the viewers from aspects of relevance and quality that might otherwise lead them to make an active response.

The core issues of relevance, quality and expense can be joined to form the set we have labelled 'actionable'. Operating from this set induces the viewers to consider whether to respond to the call to action. The attributional analysis for this set of values was quite complicated, but it does yield important suggestions about the potential use of DRTAs. Relevance was not seen as reliably present but, when it was, it was significant for the viewers, related to their own unique characteristics and led them to feel free to choose what action to take. If consideration of a DRTA got far enough for quality and expense to be relevant, these were issues located in the product or service, and in the company involved, and were therefore outside the control of the viewers. The quality issues most often considered were not required to be permanent or very significant aspects of the lives of viewers. However, if expense became an issue it was expected to have the possibility of long-term and significant consequences. Value statements in the actionable set are positive for relevance, and negative for quality and expense.

This cluster of values contains the factors that may induce viewers to phone in response to a DRTA, or may make them cautious about doing so.

Practicable implications

The research produced strong patterns that have clear implications for DRTAs. We need to say again that, because of the sample size, these are not presented as reliable guides to action. They are, however, a good indication of the capacity of attributional analysis to derive practicable implications from qualitative interviews.

1. Direct response adverts need to be very different to adverts with alternative objectives, such as creating a brand image or heightening awareness. Some aspects of advertisements make viewers appreciate them and see them as a positive aspect of their television viewing, but these aspects may work against the effectiveness of DRTAs.
2. DRTAs must establish a mental set towards taking action rather than passive enjoyment.
3. Viewers start from a position where they lose little or nothing by not responding to advertisements. DRTAs will work best if they succeed in demonstrating that they will meet the needs of the consumers. They must motivate the viewers by showing some relevance to their way of life.

4. The form and content of a DRTA must provide reassurance about trustworthiness and quality. These aspects can provide a positive incentive by giving additional reasons to want the product or service. However, they can too easily become a reason not to risk responding.

5. The content of a DRTA must, if possible, suggest a clear limit of the financial commitment entailed by responding.

6. The content of a DRTA should direct the viewers towards a mental set in which relevance, quality and price take precedence over their enjoyment of the advertisement as such. Because a DRTA must evoke a different mind set from most advertisements, it is necessary that the relevance should be stressed very early in the advertisement, before the more habitual 'appreciation' set can become established.

If these actionable implications are supported by a larger and more representative sample, several questions follow. For example:

- Does triggering an appreciation set make action calls less effective later in the ad?
- Does a DRTA provoke an action set which will carry over to a second DRTA in the same break, i.e. is the effect cumulative?
- Do factors like time of day, surrounding programme, context of viewing, affect the starting position of the viewers on the response continuum?

The factors that make the difference between whether viewers remain passive appreciators of advertisements, or take action to respond, are inevitably subtle and complex. However, once it is recognised that attributional research can identify the underlying patterns that make the difference, and relate them to specific features of advertisements, marketing can be based on sound empirical fact rather than speculation.

Having worked through three projects in some detail, we conclude by describing our experience of other consumer-oriented research. We want to show not just the variety, but also how the research fits into the requirements for good relationships reviewed at the start of the chapter. The examples are therefore organised under the headings we introduced to review issues of relationships.

ATTRIBUTIONS, RELATIONSHIPS AND CUSTOMERS' BEHAVIOUR

Perceptions

Working with utility companies, we have found the issue of visibility to be crucial. The customers want to feel that a relationship exists because the product is so crucial for them and a serious failure can be a matter of life and death. However, the product itself tends to be taken for granted and does not figure in their day-to-day thinking. It is therefore very easy for the only perception they have of the companies to be through the bills they receive and any media coverage. The media often provide coverage only when they have something negative to report. Here we have a fundamental issue in attributing: that people can only construct attributions from the information they have available. If all possible causes are negative, then only negative attributions can be selected. Because of the dependency, customers are very unforgiving. Customers can be most intolerant when they start to feel that the company is at risk of failing either because of incompetence or because it has other priorities higher than customer welfare. To identify the possibility of more positive underlying perceptions, and to specify these in ways that can be used effectively in a campaign, requires more than averagely sophisticated qualitative research.

Attraction

Attractiveness and appropriateness are not simply values that draw the customer to the product. The attributions that highlight the processes involved in purchasing decisions often incorporate them in a negative sense. People will avoid products that they judge will be seen by others as ugly, in bad taste, or pretentious. Consumers are well aware that display must be paid for, and too much attractiveness in a headquarters or an endorsement from a star can be counterproductive:

I see the ad and think 'I am paying his wages'.
So I avoid those products

Relationships do not exist in isolation, and relationship marketing must take account of how other aspects of the person's life
will impinge on the process. An example is our attributional
research on direct response TV advertisements (above). The
basic finding was that DRTAs may conflict with the relationship
that viewers normally have with advertisements. A physical response such as writing down a phone number or making a call
potentially conflicts with the dominant mode of seeing ads as a
component of the passive entertainment provided by television.
The construction of such ads must therefore be carefully specified to signal a change in relationship if they are to be effective.

The other provides interesting variations

We can offer examples from extensive research ranging from
fish to youth. British consumers say they would buy more fish if
they had recipes that tell them what to do. Yet books, news-
papers, TV programmes and magazines are full of exciting recipes for fish. The problem turns out to be that these recipes are
too far removed from the level at which most people operate.
They need to be reassured that buying and cooking fish is
simple, without traps, and reliable. Existing recipes make fish
cookery seem completely different from their existing skills, so it
is not an interesting variant, but an alien occupation. A media
campaign that was structured closely around the issues specified by the attributional analysis, and showing fish use to be a
variant on existing knowledge, has successfully produced a sus-
tained increase in fish consumption.

  A more general application of this principle is that relationship marketing needs to be based on a thorough understanding
of the customers. This enables us to know what the customers
think of the product, the brand and the company. I believe we
have to accept that customers are more complex, and more interesting, than industry currently assumes. However, too much
interest can have its own dangers. The Psychology Business decided to conduct some research as the basis for a briefing

document on the current generation of youth, which would show marketers and advertisers what is required in communicating with them (Sparham, Roy & Stratton, 1995). The document has just been completed with 20 chapters and something like a thousand practical implications identified.

CONCLUSIONS

The effect of applying the LACS to customer research has been: to extend the techniques of the research; to extend our ideas of its range of application; and to extend the perceptions of what market research can achieve. In particular, we have shown that relationship marketing can be made more effective if it attends to what has been learned from psychology's extensive studies of interpersonal relationships. Fundamental to any form of customer-oriented marketing is a detailed understanding of the customer (however defined). As the need for such understanding develops, research techniques must develop too. We see attributional analysis as one of a new breed of techniques that can meet the new demands by offering the strengths of both qualitative and quantitative methodologies. In particular: it taps directly into the core aspects of relationships, focusing on customer beliefs about cause; it can easily handle the scale and complexity of the beliefs that people hold about themselves and others who are significant to them; it can be applied with samples large enough to allow confident generalisations; and it always generates practicable solutions.

6

Future trends and research

Earlier chapters have shown the reader how the LACS method of coding and analysing causal beliefs has been applied in three broad areas of research: clinical psychology, work and organisational behaviour, and consumer beliefs and behaviour. We want to use this final chapter to speculate a little. The sections that follow describe what we think are some interesting research developments in the three key areas. In addition, we have used this opportunity to offer the reader some ideas we have concerning issues that have yet to be explored by attribution research.

ATTRIBUTIONS IN CLINICAL SETTINGS

In Chapter 3, we gave the reader a basic introduction to the role of attributions in clinical settings. We described key areas in which attribution theory has informed clinical practice and research. For many clinical psychology practitioners, finding the time and opportunity to undertake good-quality scientific research is difficult. The scientist–practitioner model, however, is increasingly advocated by many who work in clinical settings. The notion of evidence-based practice is having a significant impact on the delivery of many clinical services. Internal markets may not have been the saviours of the National Health Service, but they have encouraged managers to think very carefully about how finite resources are spent. Choices have inevitably had to be made between services that can be afforded and those that cannot. The argument that such choices should be based on evidence concerning clinical efficacy is persuasive. Why should public money be spent on treatments, such as homeopathy, for which little or no evidence concerning effectiveness exists, when the same money could be spent on funding hip replacements?

Clinical psychology is not immune to demands for empirical evidence to support claims for effective therapeutic interventions. Attribution theory can, we believe, give practitioners a powerful tool for evaluating many theories important to clinical psychology. The LACS, and other similar research tools, has the advantage of being applicable to qualitative data. Given that much of the information readily available to clinical practitioners consists of verbatim accounts of clients, making effective use of qualitative data is a major step towards collecting empirical evidence of treatment efficacy.

The value of collecting and analysing qualitative data is particularly salient when it comes to investigations concerning causal beliefs. In an influential theoretical paper, Derek Edwards and Jonathan Potter (1993) pointed out the limitations of what they called the 'classical experimental studies' of causal beliefs. You will remember from earlier chapters that most measures of attributions rely on paper and pencil tests. Typically, study participants are presented with hypothetical situations described in one or two sentences. They are then asked to attribute a cause to the outcomes described. Based on the causes provided, assumptions are made concerning specific, or sometimes habitual patterns of causal beliefs. According to Edwards and Potter, this method fails to recognise the subtlety or complexity of the relationship between language and cognition or thought. Only when causal beliefs are located within entire sequences of natural discourse can they adequately be understood. The reason is simply that people express causal beliefs for different reasons, many of which have social origins. For example, social presentation plays a significant role in determining the attributions people make. Without the rich qualitative data provided by natural discourse, contextual information needed to uncover the complexities of expressed causal beliefs is lacking. Decontextualised sentences, the mainstay of most attributional measures, are unlikely to provide sufficient or adequate information with which to determine causal beliefs. Edwards and Potter recommend that those interested in exploring attributions look at the methods and approaches used by discourse analysts, ethno-methodologists and speech act theorists.

Attributions and current clinical research

The utility of attributional analysis in clinical practice is attested to by the number of research papers identified in a trawl of the recent research literature. As an indication of the use to which researcher practitioners are putting attribution theory, and the future directions in which research may develop, we describe a selection of recently published studies in this section. The range of issues explored varies from cognitive-emotional models of helping behaviour, to parental attributions for children with cancer.

In a study of care staff responses to people with learning disabilities and challenging behaviour, Dagnan, Trower and Smith (1998) used Weiner's cognitive-emotional model of help-ing behaviour. Care staff and controls were asked to make at-tributions for examples of challenging behaviour. Beliefs concerning controllability were found to predict helping be-haviour. The authors concluded that findings may inform cognitive-behavioural approaches to working with staff beliefs and behaviour in relation to clients with challenging behaviour. The study provides a clear example of how analysis of causal beliefs has been undertaken with a clear theoretical framework. Weiner's cognitive-emotional model makes specific predictions concerning relationships between causal beliefs and behaviour that the researchers could test in an applied setting.

McKay, Chapman and Long (1996) compared causal attribu-tions made by males who had committed child sex offences, with attributions made by males convicted of either rape, prop-erty or violent offences. Based on hypotheses drawn from Weiner's (1986) theory of motivation and emotion, offenders were asked to provide causes for their offending behaviour and sexual arousal. Child sex offenders attributed their offending and sexual arousal to largely internal, stable and uncontrollable causes. Rapists and property offenders attributed their offend-ing to external, stable and internal causes, while violent offend-ers employed more internal, stable and uncontrollable explanations. All three comparison groups used external, unstable and controllable explanations for their sexual arousal. The authors concluded that their results were useful in developing cognitive therapy programmes for work with offenders of this type. Knowledge of attributions for criminal behaviour is an important first step in formulating interventions aimed at encouraging offenders to see their behaviour as changeable. Results also provided further evidence for links between attributions, emotions and behaviour as Weiner hypothesised.

MacLeod, Haynes and Sensky (1998) looked at causal attributions made by general practice patients in a study of hypochondriasis and anxiety. The aim was to look for differences between attributions patients made for health-related and non-health-related anxiety. Three groups of general practice patients were identified: anxious hypochondriacal, generally anxious, and non-anxious. All three groups were asked to provide attributions for common bodily sensations. Results showed clear group differences. Anxious patients provided more psychological and fewer normalising attributions, while hypochondriacal patients were more likely to use somatic explanations. The authors concluded that their results supported the use of attributional analysis and attributional retraining when working with these patient groups.

Building on the considerable research undertaken in the field of personal relationships, Lamm, Wiesman and Keller (1998) looked at attributions as subjective determinants of interpersonal attraction. The authors analysed written attributions made by German students for the reasons they might like, love and be in love with someone. The most frequent reasons for liking or being in love with someone concerned that person's positive attributes; for love the most frequent attributions concerned positive feelings from the other person. When it came to becoming less attracted to someone, the students reported the likely causes of liking someone less as their negative behaviour, loving someone less because of a trust betrayed, and falling out of loving because of disillusionment. The authors looked at what their results meant for theories concerning both objective and subjective determinants of interpersonal attraction and relationships.

A great deal has been written concerning the way in which we attribute motives to other people's actions, and how those attributions influence our attitudes. Fundamental attribution error, the tendency to attribute other people's behaviour to their personality rather than circumstances, is an extremely influential social phenomenon. Heyman and Gelman (1998) looked at whether children make the same kinds of trait attributions as adults when provided with similar information. Four age groups participated in the study: 5–6 year olds, 7–8 year olds, 10–11 year olds, and adults. Each group listened to short stories in which a main character, spurred on by either positive, negative or neutral motives, did something that had either positive, negative of neutral consequences for a second character. Participants were then asked why they thought the main character behaved in the way he or she did. All four age groups came up with the same trait explanations depending on how the story portrayed the main character's motives. The results provided important information for developmentalists and others working with children. Contrary to some theories of cognitive development, results suggest that children and adults use similar reasoning processes to arrive at trait explanations of behaviour. The genesis and development of attributional processes in children is still probably one of the less thoroughly researched areas in the field.

As we have already pointed out, examining attributions people make for each other's actions can provide useful information concerning the emotional dynamics of relationships. In a study of parents of children with cancer, Grootenhuis, Last, Vander Wel and DeGraaf Nijkerk (1998) looked at relationships between parental attributions and psychological adjustment. Four groups of families participated, each having a child with a different medical status: cancer in remission, cancer in relapse, asthma, and healthy. Parents of those with cancer were more likely than others to attribute cheerful behaviour to their children. However, levels of depressive symptoms reported by children in the four groups did not differ. In other words, parents of children with cancer thought their children were happier than the children said they were. The authors thought that the results might suggest that parents were using attributions as some kind of protective mechanism. Parents may find it easier to cope with their child's illness if they believe their child is coping particularly well. The results have interesting implications for clinicians helping families to cope with serious childhood illness.

On a final, more cheerful note, Dube, Jodoin and Kairouz (1998) have looked at the role of causal attributions in feelings of subjective well-being, otherwise known as happiness. Two hundred and forty participants, comprising young adults and their parents, were asked whether they attributed their happiness to internal or external causes. Most attributed their happiness to internal rather than external causes. The easier people found it to identify causes for their subjective well-being, the happier they were. Apparently the cognitive processes people go through when making subjective judgements about their well-being may hold important clues to understanding and fostering positive mental health.

It would be a mistake to conclude that hypothesised relationships between causal beliefs and psychological functioning have been verified by sound empirical evidence. As yet, the efficacy of clinical interventions aimed at shifting causal beliefs remains largely unproved. However, the examples we have discussed suggest that continued research into the role that attributions may play in the aetiology of cognitive functioning is warranted. In the experience of clinicians working at the LFTRC and elsewhere, analysis of attributions has provided some useful insights into problems brought into the clinic.

ATTRIBUTIONS IN ORGANISATIONS

In Chapter 4 we outlined three projects that had used attributional coding to explore some aspect of organisational behaviour or decision making. Many more areas and research questions could benefit from using attributional coding and in this section we would like to outline just a few. We will take two perspectives: the first is a practitioner perspective. We will discuss potential avenues that practitioners, including occupational psychologists, human resource consultants, or personnel professionals, might explore using attributional coding. The second perspective focuses on research. We will attempt to describe how attributional coding fits into organisational research, past, present and future.

The practitioner's perspective

In our experience as consultants working with organisations, the idea of attributions and attributional style has proved particularly popular. During training courses or presentations, for example, managers and trainees generally become interested very quickly in how they, and others, explain events and behaviour. People can easily identify attributions that they have heard in the media (e.g. 'the team are doing badly because their manager is lousy'), from members of the government (e.g. 'the peace agreement was reached because of exceptional mediation skills on the part of the minister'), or from colleagues and family members (e.g. 'I can't go to the office party because I have to look after the children'). In a work context, people are also motivated to listen out for attributions provided by colleagues, managers and subordinates.

In a training context, such enthusiasm is particularly rewarding and can prove an important starting point for programmes that seek to change systematically the way in which individuals think about events. One example of this is training aimed at changing the attributions often made by people who have experienced long-term unemployment. Such training has arisen because of research exploring the way in which unemployed individuals typically explain their status and their likelihood of subsequently finding work. One study by Prussia, Kinicki and Bracker (1993) looked at the attributions made by individuals who became unemployed following the closure of an engineering plant in the USA. They found that individuals who attributed their unemployment to less stable and internal causes were more likely to be employed within six months than individuals who attributed their unemployment to stable and internal causes.

Such studies have led researchers to consider whether changing the types of attributions made by individuals who have experienced long-term unemployment is possible, and if it renders these individuals more effective at seeking work. For example, if the unemployed make fewer helpless attributions, they may be more proactive in seeking work, simply because they believe that finding work is, at least in part, down to their own efforts. Training courses designed to encourage individuals to think about job-seeking behaviour and employment success in terms of more internal and controllable causes have met with some success (e.g. Proudfoot, Guest & Gray, 1994).

However, we would not suggest that attributional retraining is something that can happen easily and quickly. Nor would we argue that changing a person's attributions to a less helpless style will necessarily be the best strategy for every individual. The way in which we typically explain outcomes, our attributional style, is arguably a consequence of a lifetime of experiences and explanations. In one important respect attributional style is a strategy for coping with the difficult situations in which we find ourselves. By externalising responsibility for failure (e.g. not finding work) an individual can protect his or her self-esteem when faced with continuing experiences of failure and rejection. Moreover, the person who attributes failed attempts at securing work to external causes is, of course, in part correct, especially if that person lives in an area of high unemployment with few real opportunities for obtaining work.

Consequently, training programmes that have a simple aim of encouraging long-term unemployed people to internalise responsibility and attribute the causes of job-seeking success to more controllable causes, risk damaging an individual's self-esteem still further. This is not to say that attributional retraining is not worth while, but that, in such a situation, the task of the trainer is not so straightforward. The trainer must judge for each individual the level of perceived control that is realistic and achievable. The trainer's task is to help the individual to acknowledge his or her potential ability to control outcomes in part, without the risk of further damage to that individual's self-esteem.

As we have described in earlier chapters, clinical psychologists can use cognitive therapy to change the way in which individuals think about problems. Attributional retraining can be considered as somewhat similar. An alternative strategy for

practitioners, however, is not to attempt a complete change of
attributional style, but to raise individuals' awareness of their
own typical way of explaining outcomes related to a specific
organisational area or topic. Training is then focused on explaining how different types of attributions can have a profound
effect upon, for example, interactions with other people. Take
the example of training for customer care. Evidence suggests
that individuals differ in the extent to which they can build
successful relationships with customers and that these differences are manifest in the way in which they explain interactions with customers (Silvester & Patterson, 1998). These
differences partly result from the individual's previous experience of building relationships with family, friends and colleagues and can be used to select individuals most likely to
demonstrate excellent customer care (Patterson & Silvester,
1998).

   However, selection is only the starting point. Any further improvement in the customer care provided by these individuals
can be achieved through training focused on the attributions
that these sales assistants make for customer behaviour. Such
training can be a powerful method of raising awareness about
the way in which attributions influence the quality and success
of a relationship. It encourages the sales assistants to recognise
when they make attributions, the types of attributions they
make, and the advantages to be gained by changing the way in
which they explain events.

   One final example of how attributional coding can be useful in
a practitioner context is during projects concerned with organisational culture change. Many organisations involved in culture
change employ training programmes. Take the example of an
organisation that is introducing a 'no blame' culture. In this
culture individuals are encouraged to take ownership of problems and accept responsibility when things go wrong rather
than blame their colleagues, subordinates or managers. For
managers, blaming a subordinate for a poor result without taking proper account of their own role in creating an optimum
work environment may be all too easy. On a training course
managers can be encouraged to think through the possible
causes of the following scenario: 'One of your staff is behind

with his work and an important document that you insisted that he complete by last Friday has still not appeared.' They might also be asked to consider the consequences of expressing these different attributions to the member of staff involved. In the 'no-blame' culture encouraged by the organisation, managers might be dissuaded from simple internal attributions, that is, marking the failure down to personal inadequacies of the member of staff. They would be encouraged to identify whether they had asked too much of the individual in terms of workload, or failed to encourage the individual to prioritise, or failed to provide sufficient opportunities for training. This is not to say that a manager would never tackle a poor-performing subordinate, but merely that he or she would automatically consider other possible explanations before issuing a reprimand.

Training evaluation is an area that is frequently overlooked by organisations. However, organisations investing heavily in culture-change programmes may be more motivated to undertake evaluation to ensure that change is actually taking place. Definitions of organisational culture rely on the notion of 'shared understandings', assumptions and values held by organisational members. These are difficult to assess using pencil and paper questionnaires that usually tap into the more superficial aspects of attitudes and climate. Attributional coding, however, is one way of exploring shared understandings of why training has, or has not, been effective in achieving culture change. It can also prove useful in identifying key stakeholder groups who may be facilitating or blocking the culture change. In the study conducted by Silvester, Anderson and Patterson (in press) we found that the trainees were more positive about a culture change being introduced through a training programme than the trainers themselves!

The research perspective

Organisational research studies often rely on correlational data generated from standardised questionnaires. Indeed, a complaint commonly levied at organisational research is that it lacks a more innovative perspective. Organisational researchers seldom return to question the assumptions underlying standardised questionnaires, or consider how individuals express themselves in reality. In recent years qualitative research has gained in respectability among the research community, with many qualitative studies appearing in the, until now, entirely quantitative journals. While we applaud the increasing appreciation of qualitative research, we would also argue for the value of organisational studies that combine qualitative and quantitative perspectives. Quantitative research can benefit from a qualitative perspective just as qualitative research can from a quantitative one. Clearly, polarisation between researchers who claim either the qualitative or the quantitative moral high ground is unlikely to be productive.

Attributional coding is a method that can be used by researchers to explore the way in which people make sense of their organisational environment. It focuses on what the individual says and in this sense has excellent ecological and face validity. Attributional coding renders transparent the complex and dynamic way in which individuals explain organisational events such as mergers, acquisitions, closure of a specific function or the decision to back one product innovation rather than another. By focusing on naturalistic explanations, attributional coding provides evidence to support theorists who argue that individuals actively construct meaning and shared perspectives through interactions with others. Anyone who tries to analyse spoken attributions will certainly marvel at the complexity and dynamic forms of self-expression that different individuals use. However, the process of coding these attributions along pre-specified attributional dimensions (a quantitative perspective), enables the researcher to identify consistent and stable patterns in the attributions that individuals make for events. Thus a quantitative analysis of spoken attributions permits the exploration of consistency in 'sense-making' which allow individuals to communicate and understand one another.

Besides providing a bridge between quantitative and qualitative perspectives, attributional coding focuses organisational researchers' attention on more transactional and dynamic models of sense-making and behaviour. All too frequently researchers (and practitioners) have been satisfied with a static psychometric model of individual differences and behaviour. One example of this is the traditional 'person–job fit' model of selection. The model claims that certain static and unchanging individual qualities can be identified, such as personality and intelligence, which predict good performance on a specific job. A psychologist will then attempt to identify the individual who possesses these qualities and then appoint that person to the position. However, the traditional 'person–job fit' model has been heavily criticised in terms of its failure to address the need for flexibility both in terms of job changes and the need for the individual to develop. It also fails to take account of the considerable body of psychological literature that, in more recent years, has focused on the cognitive strategies adopted by individuals when they actively seek to understand and adapt to organisational expectancies. Attributional coding can provide some insight for the researchers interested in exploring such dynamic and proactive strategies. One area worthy of further investigation is the analysis of verbal protocol interviews in which job incumbents discuss why they have made certain decisions and taken specific courses of action. By following the same interview protocol at different times, it would be possible to track a group of individuals as they progress from novice to expert status.

To conclude, attributional coding is not a panacea to the problems faced by organisational researchers. It does force attention, however, upon the dynamic cognitive components of doing a job successfully. Attributional coding is a potentially valuable method in the researcher's tool kit—one that can provide rich rewards for the time invested in learning and becoming proficient at the method.

ATTRIBUTIONS IN CONSUMER BELIEFS AND BEHAVIOURS

Chapter 5 showed how attributional research can deal effectively with the need for industry to foster active participation by its customers. While undertaking research for many different areas of industry and public services, we have also extended the scope of the research methods far beyond their original expectations. Although this section uses marketing research as a context to describe our current thinking, the implications are applicable to all uses of the LACS.

As we consider the possibilities for extending the scope of LACS-based research even further, we are led to a much broader conceptualisation of how the relationship with the consumer influences the research process.

A variety of new approaches within psychology and beyond are giving us better ways of understanding what goes on in a research process and more realistic ways of using the results of research in practice. In taking a broader look at attributional research in consumer issues we draw on constructivist and social constructionist thinking and what has been called 'the new physics', referring to Heisenberg's Uncertainty Principle as a factor for consideration in market research (Ryan, 1986). Our starting point is captured by the agreement within British psychology to call the people who cooperate in our research 'participants' rather than 'subjects'.

Market research accepts George Kelly's insight that if you want to know what someone thinks, you should ask that person. From then on it gets less simple. One issue is the increasing sophistication of the consumer. Even 15 years ago, Lannon and Cooper (1983) pointed out that the public are now sophisticated viewers of advertisements, and can no longer be treated as passive recipients. People attribute meaning to the advertisement according to their theories of what the advertiser is trying to achieve. More recent public awareness of market research itself, especially the political use of focus groups, creates an urgent need to rethink the whole research process. In particular, we need to build into our accounts of research the theories and understanding of all of the participants.

A key issue to consider is how these changes affect the relative merits of qualitative and quantitative research. Quantitative research suffers from a variety of limitations. Some derive from the problems that arise when a standardised questionnaire is offered to a respondent who may not share the same meanings as the researcher and who may have little investment to provide accurate information. Many quantitative methods lack the scope to ensure that data are meaningful. Nor is there a demand characteristic of the situation that would lead either researcher or interviewee to negotiate an optimal meaning. The fact that standardised questionnaire items have to be constructed and subjected to extensive development and refinement before data are gathered is the other major limitation. It means that the scope of the data is fixed before the research starts, rather than being an outcome of the research.

One way of dealing with this problem is to start with qualitative research to define issues, and build questionnaires on the results. However, within market research, this solution is made ineffective by the limitations in the role given to qualitative methods. Without a technique like attributional analysis, qualitative research can become little more than a way of supporting the insights that the researcher already created.

In an interview, the respondents are free to express themselves in their own words. Consequently, they are likely to have made a greater commitment because of the length of the interview and the face-to-face nature of the information gathering. The main problems created by open interviews are those of analysis. Because the material gathered is partly under the control of the interviewee, it has to be interpreted. It is our contention that it is this process of interpretation that is the core of past limitations in qualitative market research and it is here that the LACS makes its greatest contribution. Accounts of marketing research, such as Weiers (1988), describe a variety of methods used to improve the quality of information from qualitative interviews. In essence these move either towards quantitative methods (for example, attitude scaling within the interview) or towards material that exacerbates the problems of interpretation, as with projective techniques. Typically, Weiers gives almost no consideration of the issue of how the interview material is to be analysed. Interviews are treated in such texts as if the problem was merely a matter of getting the interviewee to provide the material. However, a quite basic job will consist of four groups lasting more than one hour, and with six or eight respondents in each group. If the issue is particularly important, many more groups may be required. One of our studies required 200 one-hour interviews. The size and careful specification of the sample enabled us to generalise the conclusions to the relevant population. However, with any other method the sheer amount of material generated, even with all the interviews transcribed, would have been unmanageable.

The researcher will typically reduce interview material to a set of notes that are then used as an intermediate phase on the way to a final report. The process involves a considerable amount of interpretation, of selection, and of creative insight. Unfortunately all of these processes reduce the replicability of the findings that eventually emerge. Until recently few serious attempts to develop techniques for the analysis of verbatim material have been made. None of the applications of content analysis suggests a sufficiently fine-grained approach that would meet the needs of marketing research. As for computerised word searches, our own experience is that natural language is so far from any form of language structure that a computer can recognise, that a word search, even at the level of sophistication allowed by the Oxford Concordance Package, will pick up less than 50% of the material that a human being will identify.

Computerisation has its dangers of mystification. The fact that interviews are now routinely transcribed using word processors, so that the text can be entered for processing with little effort has encouraged some poor research. In essence these attempts amount to word searches, either looking for patterns in the frequency of use of words by respondents, or else identifying phrases by the occurrence of words or combinations of words. This contrasts with the theory-driven approach of attributional analysis that provides a powerful and well-specified framework for choosing, coordinating and interpreting the content of a discussion.

The lack of powerful and efficient techniques for analysing interviews has resulted in major limitations in the scope of qualitative research. The first point is that the limitations on techniques for analysing qualitative material has meant that only limited use of open-ended interview material has been possible. Typically Qualitative Market Research (QMR) interviews have been treated as sources of ideas and as checks that assumptions were not wildly inaccurate. Because of this limited use, there has been no requirement that data obtained through interviews should be representative, as long as the people sampled are broadly in the right categories.

The chronically poor sampling that this has led to in QMR has, in turn, created a belief that results cannot and should not be generalised. However then, because results will not be generalised, there is no need to take too much care over sampling. The whole industry risks being caught up in a vicious cycle in which the limitations of qualitative methods in the past cause low expectations, demanding low standards (and costs) of research, thus confirming the low expectations.

We would propose that a constructionist perspective could be used to rethink the entire enterprise of QMR. For many researchers the process is seen as an objective search for hard facts that can then be inserted into the subsequent stages of marketing strategy through to advertising and sales. If, instead, we see the interview (individual or group) as a process of creating shared meaning, we are immediately forced to attend to the reality of the research process. Attributions are not best treated as reports of causal beliefs that have an independent existence inside the head of the respondent. They are phenomena created by the context and have to be interpreted in that way.

At its most basic, this means that the content of an interview will be strongly influenced by the demand characteristics of the situation. The respondents will assess the requirements of the situation and, at every level, will adjust their communication to fit. We can make this an advantage rather than a disadvantage. We lose the idea of the transcript as containing an objective description of reality, but in exchange we obtain a great improvement in our ability to increase the richness of our material.

Thinking of the respondents as active participants, acting in terms of that other participant the interviewer, focuses attention on the processes that guide the choice of what is communicated in the interview. If the contribution of the interviewer, and the interview context and structure can be taken into account, one can use the amount of explanation offered by the respondents as indicative of the role and importance of the issue to them. This is the core of the attributional approach.

People will attempt to produce explanations only when they feel that their existing explanations are inadequate. Encountering an expected event does not produce any tendency to attempt to explain it. In a conversation, it is the judgement that the event is unexpected for the other person that triggers the attempt to supply an explanation.

The idea here corresponds closely to the account of 'scripts' offered by Schank and Abelson (1977) following their attempts to program computers to track the kinds of accounts offered by people. They suggest that when two people share an understanding of the expected features of a situation, these features will not be mentioned. For example, we all have a script for the processes involved in having a meal in a restaurant. So an account might consist of saying, 'We went to The Flying Pizza last night and my friend left a big tip.' There is no need to mention that you were offered a menu, chose, were served, ate, paid the bill and so on, because this is shared information about 'the restaurant script'. However, any deviation from the script is highly likely to be mentioned. If you had not eaten, or had got out without paying the bill, you would know that the listener would not assume either fact, and that if you wanted them to know precisely what had happened you would need to tell them these aspects.

So there seem to be two primary conditions that will make it likely that an explanation will be offered: a belief that the other participant does not possess the information, and a wish that they should understand. These are added to the requirement to establish a definable context in which the relevant part of the consumer's meaning system becomes activated and accessible to the interviewer. So the key to the form of interview that we need is to set up a situation in which:

- a shared meaning will be created;
- the respondent will want to provide explanations;
- the respondent will assume a lack of knowledge in the interviewer.

This approach generates the data we need for an attributional analysis. It also allows us to make explicit the role of the interviewer in the creation of shared meaning, so that an unambiguous interpretation of the respondents' explanations is possible. The nature of attributional research makes it ideal for this approach. The interview creates accounts of relevant aspects of the lives of the respondents, in which it is precisely those aspects that are relevant in their choices of action that are prioritised. They will spend less time talking about habitual and obvious processes, and the data will reflect the beliefs and expectations that they judge to be of concern to themselves and the interviewer. As we have built on the techniques of the LACS we have become aware of how important it is to define the context of the discussion. Within a conversation, people talk at different levels of context, prioritising different concerns at different times. Let us take an exploration of branding as an example.

The consumers will have a set of meanings concerning the product and how they use it. They may have a perception of the manufacturer, and a more specific judgement about the particular product. For example, they may regard canned soup as a useful standby food; Heinz as a company associated with quality ingredients; but Heinz tomato soup as tasting nice. Then there are the different contexts in which they might think about using canned soup: as a parent, a spouse, a busy worker, a person with certain needs, a person who wants the best, or is economical, or is not conned by advertisements, or is different from their parents, or does not waste time making trivial decisions. It is only through a coherent analysis of the construction of meaning between the consumers, and the ways that different sources of information affect these varied levels of context, that a meaningful description of the brand position, and a judgement about the consequences of a particular advertising strategy, can be useful.

Attributional research enables us to move away from simplistic notions of the person as a simple container of attitudes. Which is just as well since attitudes are rather poor predictors of behaviour. Current developments in applying the constructionist perspective within psychology point the way to further developments of the LACS. We can hope to see a whole way of thinking about research that eliminates the boundary between qualitative and quantitative methods and which, because we can capture the richness of thinking of consumers, encourages industry to cope with the complexity of their relationship with their customers.

References

Abramson, L.Y., Seligman, M.E.P. & Teasdale, J. (1978). Learned help-lessness in humans: Critique and reformulation. *Journal of Abnormal Psychology*, **87**, 49–74.

Bell, R.Q. (1979). Parent, child and reciprocal influences. *American Psychologist*, **34**, 821–826.

Borden, K.A. & Brown, R.T. (1989). Attributional Outcomes: The subtle message of treatments for Attention Deficit Disorder. *Cognitive Therapy and Research*, **13**, 147–160.

Bowlby, J. (1969). *Attachment*. London: Hogarth Press.

Bowlby, J. (1988). *A Secure Base*. London: Basic Books.

Brewin, C.R. (1985). Depression and causal attributions: What is their relation? *Psychological Bulletin*, **98**, 297–309.

Dagnan, D., Trower, P. & Smith, R. (1998). Care staff responses to people with learning disabilities and challenging behaviour: A cognitive-emotional analysis. *British Journal of Clinical Psychology*, **37**, 59–68.

Deal, T.E. & Kennedy, A.A. (1982). *Corporate Cultures: The Rites and Rituals of Corporate Life*. Reading, MA: Addison Wesley.

Dube, L., Jodoin, M. & Kairouz, S. (1998). On the cognitive basis of subjective well-being analysis: What do individuals have to say about it? *Canadian Journal of Behavioural Science*, **30**, 1–13.

Edwards, D. & Potter, J. (1993). Language and causation: A discursive action model of description and attribution. *Psychological Review*, **100**, 23–41.

Fincham, F. (1994). Cognition in marriage: Current status and future challenges. *Applied and Preventive Psychology*, **3**, 185–198.

Fincham, F., Beach, S.R. & Baucom, D.H. (1987). Attribution processes in distressed and nondistressed couples: 4. Self-partner attribution differences. *Journal of Personality and Social Psychology*, **52**, 739–748.

Fincham, F., Fernandes, L.O., & Humphreys, K.H. (1993). *Communicating in Relationships: A Guide for Couples and Professionals*. Champaign, IL: Research Press.

Fosterling, F. (1988). *Attribution Theory in Clinical Psychology*. New York: Wiley.

Furnham, A., Sadka, V. & Brewin, C.R. (1992). The development of an occupational attributional style questionnaire. *Journal of Organizational Behaviour*, **13**, 27–39.

Gewirtz, J.L. (1972). *Attachment and Dependency*. Washington, DC: Winston.

Grootenhuis, M.A., Last, B.F., Vander Wel, M., & DeGraaf Nijkerk, J.H. (1998). Parents' attributions of positive characteristics to their children with cancer. *Psychology and Health*, **13**, 67–81.

Heider, F. (1958). *The Psychology of Interpersonal Relations*. New York: Wiley.

Herriot, P. (1989). Attribution theory and interview decisions. In M. Smith & I.T. Robertson (Eds), *The Employment Interview: Theory, Research and Practice*. London: Sage.

Heyman, G.D. & Gelman, S.A. (1998). Young children use motive information to make trait inferences. *Developmental Psychology*, **34**, 310–321.

Hobbs, C., Hanks, H. & Wynne, J. (1993). *Child Abuse and Neglect: A Clinician's Handbook*. London: Churchill Livingston.

Hofstede, G. (1991). *Cultures and Organizations: Intercultural Cooperation and its Importance for Survival*. London: HarperCollins.

Holtzworth-Munroe, A. & Jacobsen, N.S. (1985). Causal attributions in married couples: When do they search for causes? What do they conclude when they do? *Journal of Personality and Social Psychology*, **48**, 1398–1412.

Jones, E.E. & Davis, K.E. (1965). A theory of correspondent inferences: From Acts to Dispositions. In L. Berkowitz (Ed.), *Advances in Experimental Social Psychology*, Vol. 2, New York: Academic Press.

Joseph, S.A., Brewin, C.R., Yule, W. & Williams, R. (1993). Causal attributions and post- traumatic stress in adolescents. *Journal of Child Psychology and Psychiatry*, **34**, 247–253.

Kelley, H.H. (1973). The process of causal attribution. *American Psychologist*, **28**, 107–128.

Kulik, C.T. & Rowland, K.M. (1989). The relationship of attributional frameworks to job seekers' perceived success and job search involvement. *Journal of Organizational Behaviour*, **10**, 361–367.

Lamm, H., Weisman, U. & Keller, K. (1998). Subjective determinants of attraction: Self-perceived causes of the rise and decline of liking, love, and being in love. *Personal Relationships*, **5**, 91–104.

Lannon, J. & Cooper, P. (1983). Humanistic advertising: A holistic cultural perspective. *International Journal of Advertising*, **2**, 195–213.

Larrance, D.T. & Twentyman, C.T. (1983). Maternal attributions and child abuse. *Journal of Abnormal Psychology*, **92**, 449–457.

Lewin, K. (1948). *Resolving Social Conflicts*. New York: Harper.

MacLeod, A.K., Haynes, C. & Sensky, T. (1998). Attributions about common bodily sensations: Their associations with hypochondriasis and anxiety. *Psychological Medicine*, **28**, 225–228.

McCann, J.B., Stein, A., Fairburn, C.G. & Dunger, D.B. (1994). Eating habits and attitudes of mothers of children with No-ftt. *Archives of Diseases in Childhood*, **70**, 234–236.

McKay, M., Chapman, J.W. & Long, N.R. (1996). Causal attributions for criminal offending and sexual arousal: Comparison of child sex offenders with other offenders. *British Journal of Clinical Psychology*, **35**, 63–75.

Mischel, W. (1968). *Personality and Assessment*. New York: Wiley.

Mischel, W. (1973). Toward a cognitive social learning reconceptualization of personality. *Psychological Review*, **80**, 252–283.

Parry, G. & Brewin, C.R. (1988). Cognitive style and depression: Symptom-related, event-related, or independent provoking factor? *British Journal of Clinical Psychology*, **27**, 19–31.

Patterson, F.M. & Silvester, J. (1998). Counter measures. *People Management*, **4**(9), 46–48.

Payne, A. (1998). *Relationship Marketing for Competitive Advantage: Winning and Keeping Customers*. Oxford: Butterworth Heinemann.

Payne, A. (1995). *Advances in Relationship Marketing*. London: Kogan Page.

Proudfoot, J., Guest, D. & Gray, J.A. (1994). Attributional retraining and the unemployed. Paper presented at the British Psychological Society Annual Occupational Psychology Conference, Birmingham.

Prussia, G.E., Kinicki, A.J. & Bracker, J.S. (1993). Psychological and behavioral consequences of job loss: A covariance structure analysis using Weiner's (1985) attribution model. *Journal of Applied Psychology*, **78**, 382–394.

Quadrel, M.J. & Lau, R.R. (1989). Health promotion, health locus of control, and health behaviour: two field experiments. *Journal of Applied Social Psychology*, **19**, 1497–1521.

Ryan, M. (1986) Implications from the 'Old' and the 'New' physics for studying buyer behaviour. In D. Brinberg & R. Lutz (Eds), *Perspective on Methodology in Consumer Research*. New York: Springer-Verlag.

Schank, R. & Abelson, R. (1977). *Scripts, Plans, Goals, and Understanding*. Hillsdale, NJ: Erlbaum.

Schein, E.H. (1985). *Organisational Culture and Leadership*. San Francisco: Jossey Bass.

Schulman, P., Castellon, C. & Seligman, M.E.P. (1989). Assessing explanatory style: The content analysis of verbatim explanations and the Attributional Style Questionnaire. *Behaviour Research Therapy*, **27**, 505–512.

Silvester, J. (1997). Spoken attributions and candidate success in graduate recruitment interviews. *Journal of Occupational and Organizational Psychology*, **70**, 61–73.

Silvester, J. (1989). Causal attribution in distressed and non-distressed parent–child relationships. Unpublished PhD thesis, University of Leeds.

Silvester, J. & Chapman, A.J. (1996). Unfair discrimination in the selection interview: an attributional account. *International Journal of Selection and Assessment*, **4**, 63–70.

Silvester, J., Anderson, N.R. & Patterson, F.M. (in press). Organisational culture change: An inter-group attributional analysis. *Journal of Occupational and Organizational Psychology*.

Silvester, J., Bentovim, A., Stratton, P. & Hanks, H.G.I. (1995). Using spoken attributions to classify abusive families. *Child Abuse and Neglect*, **19**, 1221–1232.

Silvester, J., Ferguson, E. & Patterson, F. (1997). A cross cultural comparison of the attributions produced by German and UK engineers. *European Journal of Work and Organizational Psychology*, **6**, 103–117.

Silvester, J. & Patterson, F.M. (1998). Selecting successful sales staff. Paper presented at the International Work Psychology Conference, Sheffield.

Snyder, C.R. & Higgins, R.L. (1988). Excuses: Their effective role in the negotiation of reality. *Psychological Bulletin*, **104**, 23–35.

Sparham, E., Roy, J. & Stratton, P. (1995). Youth: The voice of a lost generation. *Human Systems*, **6**, 295–308.

Stratton, P. (1991) Attributions, baseball, and consumer behaviour. *Journal of the Market Research Society*, **33**, 163–178.

Stratton, P. (1995a). Systemic interviewing and attributional analysis applied to international broadcasting. In J. Haworth (Ed.), *Psychological Research: Innovative Methods and Strategies*. London: Routledge.

Stratton, P. (1995b). Causal processes determining the effectiveness of direct response television advertisements, *Journal of Targeting, Measurement and Analysis for Marketing*, **4**, 212–222.

Stratton, P. (1997) Attributional coding of interview data. In N. Hayes (Ed.), *Doing Qualitative Analysis in Psychology*. Hove, East Sussex: Psychology Press.

Stratton, P., Munton, A.G., Hanks, H., Heard, D.H. & Davidson, C. (1988). *Leeds Attributional Coding System (LACS) Manual*. Leeds: LFTRC.

Sturm, L. & Drotar, D. (1989). Prediction of weight for height following intervention in three year old children with early histories of non-organic failure-to-thrive. *Child Abuse and Neglect*, **13**, 19–28.

Tajfel, H. (1982). *Human Groups and Social Categories*. Cambridge: Cambridge University Press.

Trice, H.M. & Beyer, J.M. (1984). Studying organisational culture through rites and rituals. *Academy of Management Review*, **9**, 653–669.

Weiers, R.M. (1988) *Marketing Research* (2nd Edn) New Jersey: Prentice Hall.

Weiner, B. (1985). Spontaneous causal thinking. *Psychological Bulletin*, **97**, 74–84.

Weiner, B. (1986). *An Attributional Theory of Motivation and Emotion*. New York: Springer-Verlag.

Wells, G.L. (1981). Lay analyses of causal forces on behaviour. In J.H. Harvey (Ed.), *Cognition, Social Behaviour and the Environment*. Hillsdale, NJ: Erlbaum.

Further reading

Antaki, C.R. (1988). *Analyzing Everyday Explanation: A Casebook of Methods*. London: Sage.

Antaki, C.R. (1994). *Explaining and Arguing*. London: Sage.

Baucom, D.H. (1987). Attributions in distressed relationships: How can we explain them? In D. Perlman & S. Duck (Eds), *Intimate Relationships: Development, Dynamics and Deterioration*. London: Sage.

Brewin, C.R., MacCarthy, B., Duda, K. & Vaughn, C.E. (1991). Attribution and expressed emotion in the relatives of families with schizophrenia. *Journal of Abnormal Psychology*, **100**, 546–554.

Brewin, C.R. & Shapiro, D.A. (1984). Beyond locus of control: Attribution of responsibility for positive and negative outcomes. *British Journal of Psychology*, **75**, 43–50.

Corr, P.J. & Gray, J.A. (1996). Attributional style as a personality factor in insurance sales performance in the UK. *Journal of Occupational and Organizational Psychology*, **69**, 83–87.

Doise, W. (1980). Levels of explanation. *European Journal of Social Psychology*, **10**, 213–231.

Fincham, F. & Jaspars, J. (1979). Attributions of responsibility to the self and other in children and adults. *Journal of Personality and Social Psychology*, **37**, 1589–1602.

Fleiss, J.L. (1971). Measuring nominal scale agreement among many raters. *Psychological Bulletin*, **76**, 378–382.

Forster, N. (1994). The Analysis of Company Documentation. In C. Cassell & G. Symon (Eds), *Qualitative Methods in Organizational Research. A Practical Guide*. London: Sage.

Furnham, A., Brewin, C.R. & O'Kelly, H. (1994). Cognitive style and attitudes to work. *Human Relation*, **47**, 1509–1521.

Harris, M.M. (1989). Reconsidering the employment interview: A review of recent literature and suggestions for future research. *Personnel Psychology*, **42**, 691–726.

Harvey, J.H., Turnquist, D.C. & Agostinelli, G. (1988). Identifying attributions in oral and written explanations in C. Antaki (Ed.), *Analyzing Everyday Explanation: A Casebook of Methods*. London: Sage.

King, N. (1994). The qualitative research interview. In C. Cassell & G. Symon (Eds), *Qualitative Methods in Organizational Research. A Practical Guide*. London: Sage.

Kipnis, D.S., Schmidt, K., Price, K. & Stitt, C. (1981). Why do I like thee: Is it your performance or my orders? *Journal of Applied Psychology*, **66**, 324–328.

Knowlton, W.A. & Mitchell, T.R. (1980). Effects of causal attributions on a supervisor's evaluation of subordinate performance. *Journal of Applied Psychology*, **65**, 459–466.

Marshall, H. (1994). Discourse analysis in an organizational context. In C. Cassell & G. Symon (Eds.), *Qualitative Methods in Organizational Research. A Practical Guide*. London: Sage.

Munton, A.G. & Antaki, C. (1988). Causal beliefs amongst families in therapy. *British Journal of Clinical Psychology*, **27**, 91–98.

Peterson, C. & Seligman, M.E.P. (1984). Causal explanations as a risk factor for depression: Theory and evidence. *Psychological Review*, **91**, 347–374.

Peterson, C., Semmel, A., Von Baeyer, C., Abramson, L.Y., Metalsky, G.I. & Seligman, M.E.P. (1982). The Attributional Style Questionnaire. *Cognitive Therapy and Research*, **6**, 287–300.

Prussia, G.E., Kinicki, A.J. & Bracker, J.S. (1993). Psychological and behavioural consequences of job loss: A covariance structure analysis using Weiner's (1985) attribution model. *Journal of Applied Psychology*, **78**, 382–394.

Rousseau, D.M. (1990). Assessing organisational culture: the case for multiple methods. In B. Schneider (Ed.), *Organisational Climate and Culture*. San Francisco: Jossey Bass.

Seligman, M.E.P. & Schulman, C. (1986). Explanatory style as a predictor of productivity and quitting among life insurance sales agents. *Journal of Personality and Social Psychology*, **50**, 832–838.

Silvester, J., Patterson, F., Anderson, N. & Ferguson, E. (1995). Unlocking the quality culture: A socio-cognitive model of organisational culture and culture change. *Proceedings of the British Psychological Society Occupational Psychology Conference*, Warwick.

Stratton, P., Heard, D., Hanks, H.G.I., Munton, A.G., Brewin, C.R. & Davidson, C. (1986). Coding causal beliefs in natural discourse. *British Journal of Social Psychology*, **25**, 299–313.

Sujan, H. (1986). Smarter versus harder: An exploratory attributional analysis of sales people's motivation. *Journal of Marketing Research*, **23**, 41–49.

Wong, P.T.P. & Weiner, B. (1981). When people ask 'why' questions and the heuristics of attribution search. *Journal of Personality and Social Psychology*, **40**, 649–663.

Index

relationships
    attraction 177–9
    basic requirements 145–8
    and customers' behaviour 177–9
    definition 144–5
    perceptions 177
reliability of data 7–9, 34
retailing 143
role-play 31
Rotter 16

salespeople
    attributional style 108
    customer care 124, 127–9
    interpersonal attributions 108–9
    performance of 123
    sales outcomes 122–4
    sales performance 125–7
scripts 196
selection 188
self-blame attributions 82
self-serving bias 111, 131
Seligman, Martin 14, 15, 31, 47, 75,
        108, 123
sense-making 114
sexual abuse 43, 98, 101–2, 182
Skinner, B.F. 3
social identity theory 148
social learning theory 13–14, 16
social referencing 148
speech act theory 182
spoken attributions, limitations of 103
Statistical Package for the Social
        Sciences (SPSS) 33, 59
stimulus–response learning (S-R) 5
stimulus–stimulus learning (S-S) 5
strategic impression management
        115
subjective well-being, causal
        attribution of 185
superego 4
supervisor attributions for employee
        behaviour 109–11

symptom model 76

telephone cold-calling 124
television 167–77
    core issues 169–75
    practicable implications 175–7
    procedures 168–9
therapeutic intervention, attributions
        and 80–6
Total Quality Management (TQM)
        131
training evaluation 189
trait explanations of behaviour 184
transference 143

ultimate attributional bias 112
unemployment 186–7
utilities 142–3

violent offences 182
vulnerability model 76

Weiner 15–16, 18
workplace attributions
    at individual level 107–8
    at interpersonal level 108–11
    case examples of coding 116–37
    customer care 124, 127–9
    importance of 105–16
    intergroup attributions 111–13
    limitations of method 137–8
    organisational attributions 113–16,
        129–37
        actual–hypothetical 133–4
        agent–target 132
        global–specific 133
        positive–negative 132
        results 134–7
        stable–unstable 133
    sales outcomes 122–4
    sales performance 125–7
    selection interview 32, 117–22,
        188

Index compiled by Annette Musker